CAREERS IN RELIGIOUS COMMUNICATIONS

OTHER BOOKS ON COMMUNICATIONS BY THE SAME AUTHOR

Interpreting the Church Through Press and Radio
Understanding Magazines
The Magazine World
The Changing Magazine
Critical Writing for the Journalist
The Journalist's Bookshelf
The Black Press, U.S.A.

In Collaboration
Exploring Journalism (with Laurence R. Campbell)
Newsmen at Work (with Laurence R. Campbell)
How to Report and Write the News (with Laurence R. Campbell)
Writing for the Religious Market (Editor and Coauthor)
The Copyreader's Workshop (with Harry F. Harrington)
Around the Copydesk (with George C. Bastian and Leland D. Case)
New Survey of Journalism (with George Fox Mott and others)
Journalism Tomorrow (with Wesley C. Clark and others)
Perspectives of the Black Press, 1974 (with Henry G. La Brie III and others)
Journalism in Modern India (Editor and Coauthor)

OTHER BOOKS
The Low Countries
Face to Face with India
Gandhi: Warrior of Non-Violence (with P. D. Tandon)
Three Women to Remember (with P. D. Tandon)

CAREERS IN RELIGIOUS COMMUNICATIONS

Roland E. Wolseley
Professor Emeritus of Journalism
School of Public Communications
Syracuse University

Third Edition

HERALD PRESS
Scottdale, Pennsylvania
Kitchener, Ontario

CAREERS IN RELIGIOUS COMMUNICATIONS (Third Edition)
Copyright 1955 by National Board of Young Men's Christian Association
Copyright © 1966, 1977 by Herald Press, Scottdale, Pa. 15683
  Published simultaneously in Canada by Herald Press,
  Kitchener, Ont. N2G 4M5
Library of Congress Catalog Card Number: 66-27707
International Standard Book Number: 0-8361-1823-5
Printed in the United States of America
Design: Alice B. Shetler

10 9 8 7 6 5 4 3 2 1

To My Mother

Whose Gifts of Books about Journalism
Started Me, During My Boyhood, Along
My Own Path in That Occupation

Contents

Prayer for a Writer — 8
Preface to the Third Edition — 9
1 Communications as a Vocation — 13
2 Communications as a Religious Vocation — 26
3 The Job Situation — 44
4 On the Secular Job — 69
5 On the Religious Job — 91
6 Publicists of Religion — 118
7 The Missionary Communicators — 136
8 Foreign Correspondent-Priest Tells His Story
   By James P. Colligan, MM — 156
9 Free-Lance Writers About Religion — 169
10 Preparing for and Starting a Career — 194
Index — 237
The Author — 239

Prayer for a Writer*

By Harry Franklin Harrington

Help me, O Lord, in a land of borrowed ideas to keep and develop what originality I already possess.

Make me more aggressive, more interested and alert in my daily contacts with people and with life, that I may find fresh material on which to write.

Increase, O Lord, my power to observe and feel and think, and to express my inmost thoughts with daring, incisiveness, and pungency.

Forgive my indifferent spelling and my careless literary lapses, and prune my manuscript of faded phrases and dangling sentences.

Give me the courage to say resolutely, "I don't know," and then to go out unashamed to discover the right answer.

Help me to cultivate constantly at least one major interest, and to enjoy at least one recreation and hobby.

Give me an abiding pleasure in the arduous task of writing, keeping in mind always my obligation to win the interest of my reader.

Keep my mind well filled but never closed, and free me of conceit, buncombe, and pose, so that I may do my daily stint honestly and thoroughly, and without too much expectation of applause.

Let me not be too greatly discouraged by rejection slips, remembering that acceptance cometh in the morning.

And when my typewriter is covered with dust, O Lord, add to my unfinished story a happy ending to all I have dreamed and thought and prayed. *Amen*

---

*Reproduced by permission from *Modern Feature Writing*, by Harry F. Harrington and Elmo Scott Watson. Harper and Brothers, New York, 1935.

Preface to the Third Edition

One of my major reasons for writing this book is the hope that it will find its way into the hands of persons of any ages interested in working in the communications field but unsure of what they need to bring to it and what the problems are for the person of religious convictions.

It is intended for the use, also, of vocational counselors, the clergy, and other persons who can channel gifted and sincere men and women into religious work in secular communications or into any phase of religious communications.

The media of mass communications never have been so important and so powerful as they now are. Religious persons must know how to make use of them as consumers of their output and as employees, actual or prospective, know how to be effective workers. But they cannot do so unless they understand the media and, as workers, are trained well and gain proper experience.

This book can only point to the possibilities, explain what the different jobs are like, give an idea of the working conditions and salaries, tell about some of the persons who have found places in the field, and beat the drum for more recruits to an influential and significant field for religious service. Many other books explain the techniques, the historical background, and the philosophy of the American type of communications of which that of religion is a part. There is no need to repeat them. Some of these volumes should be read and accompanied by training and experience. But no other recent book has tried to depict the particular specialized area known as religious communications from the vocational standpoint; that may be the unique contribution of *Careers in Religious Communications*.

Many changes have been made for this new edition, beginning with the title, which originally was *Careers in Religious Journalism*. During the twenty years of life for the two earlier editions the word *communications* has come more and more to supersede *journalism*. It has become an umbrella-like term embracing journalism, since the latter generally is thought to involve only printed communications. Career stories have been updated where possible; a dozen new ones have been added and highlighted by separate presentation. Considerable new information about each aspect of religious communications has been added as well. The reading lists have been amplified, and all photographs are new.

Long lists of acknowledgments would be cumbersome in a book so short as this. Most of the living persons referred to here have cooperated by providing recent facts on their careers. Various others have given wise counsel and supplied facts.

I am particularly grateful to the score of busy editors, public information office directors, and other religious communications officials who responded to questions put to them about the trends and the job situation. Their names appear with quotations from their replies in three summaries of the study results found in chapters 3 and 10.

Roland E. Wolseley
Syracuse, N.Y.
December 1976

The opportunities for careers in religious service through communication, in my view, will soar in the next decade.

Wilmer C. Fields
Director of Public Relations
Executive Committee
Southern Baptist Convention

1 Communications as a Vocation

What Shall I Do with My Life?

That question enters and reenters the minds of sensitive young persons, whether they are in high school, in college, or on a job. But it also, at times, occurs to many a mature man or woman who apparently is well settled in life but perhaps through a religious experience is moved to evaluate his or her service in the world.

Whatever the questioner's age, sex, or condition, his or her first thought rarely is to answer by saying: "I shall aid mankind by serving through communications." More likely to come to mind is the ministry, the mission field, or nursing.

Not to think of the media—much less the media of religion—at first is natural. For the idea of a vocation in communications is a relatively new one, communications itself being a comparatively young profession. Its religious aspects are even newer. Although church papers and magazines have been published for well more than a century in the United States and Canada, only in recent years have careers on their staffs become attractive. To them have been added other career possibilities growing out of the development of modern communications. These are in religious broadcasting and film, public relations, publicity, advertising, and missionary journalism, among others discussed in this book.

What Is Communication?

The term, communication, has a general meaning. It has been simply defined by Neal and Brown, in their book, *Newswriting and Reporting,* as "the transmission or exchange of information or ideas or feelings by means of sounds, signs, or symbols." They define mass communication, in a way which follows logically, as "the transmission of information to large numbers of persons, usually over a considerable geographical area."

Another term which requires classification before we go further is *religious.*[1] Among some communicators who deal with religion as a subject exists the opinion that they should be called *religion communicators* (or *religion* news writers, *religion* reporters, *religion* editors, and the like) rather than *religious news writers,* or *religious journalists.* They are right, literally, because a person writing about religion is not necessarily religious. Sportswriters often are poor athletes but may win prizes for their writing just the same. Medical journalists are not often doctors nor science writers scientists.

But the terms religious journalist, religious communi-

cators, and the like have become so fixed in the language that we shall use them in this book for the sake of communication if not literal accuracy.

The Lure of Communications

In the United States and Canada, communications as a career has been attractive for many years. Newspapers, magazines, and broadcasting stations never lack applicants. In recent years, because of the interpretive reporting done by communications people, the schools of journalism and communications have been flooded with young people eager to enter the field.

Why is it so attractive? Why does work as a reporter, photojournalist, editor, or broadcaster seem appealing? Journalism and communications have had this lure all through their histories, particularly the former. It was true even in the days when it paid its employees badly and gave them no security. Its magnetism has several explanations.

Communications is self-expression. In a society becoming more and more mechanized, leaving more operations than ever before to calculators and computers, communications remains a place for the individual to be creative, even though more and more of the work is being done by electronic means. The reporter for any medium takes news in the raw and designs a news story to be read over the air or printed. The photographer imprisons events on his film. The article writer combines facts and ideas into a unit of writing born in her brain. In its magazine form, communications is a storehouse of short stories, poems, and other imaginative work. Hundreds of the world's leading literary people were or still are journalists or some other kind of communicator.

Communications is popular education. For many persons it is the only school, a living textbook, teaching its readers, listeners, and viewers history, economics, homemaking, and dozens of other subjects. It appeals to the desire to inform possessed by most of us. But it appeals especially to the communicator, who sometimes is part preacher, part teacher.

Communications is exciting. In its news aspects, especially, it is exciting, fast-moving, and blood-quickening. People in communications appear to be possessed of second sight. They are ahead of the news, behind the scenes of events, and inside the inside information. All phases of journalistic and communications work are related to life about us, for they are concerned with now as well as with the future. Communications deals with ever-changing situations.

Communications is power. The editor of a small country weekly exerts the power of the press in his hamlet, and so does the publisher of a big metropolitan daily in his city. The newspaper press has made and broken governments, designed legislation, exposed lawbreakers, and insisted upon social reforms. It also has turned publicized nonentities into international figures and made the trivial seem important. However used, its power appeals to the desire to exert leadership. Electronic communications influences elections, moves industrial products and services, educates the public, and fixes lifestyles.

Communications is more than all this, as we shall see elsewhere in this book. Religious communications is a part of it, but its relationship will be better understood when we examine briefly the background into which it fits today, the meaning of vocation, and the spiritual force inherent in the occupation.

The Scope of Communications

People often are mistaken about what communications includes. The casual answer is that it has something to do with telegraphy and telephony. It is far more than that. It also covers newspapers, magazines, broadcasting, film, theater, newsletters, books, billboards, other forms of advertising, photography, printing, signal systems, and every other way of exchanging or projecting messages. Such communications falls into two classes: public (or mass) and private. Messages disseminated by way of newspapers, magazines, radio, television, photography, cassettes, recordings, tapes, film, and theater are for all citizens; the rest are communications between individuals. The mass media can be restricted to individual use, as for example a cassette made by a brother to be heard by another brother elsewhere, but generally speaking the public media have far wider use as mass communications.

The word *media* has become increasingly important in the communications world. It is given to much misuse. One means of communication, the radio for instance, is a medium; when two or more means of mass communication are under discussion they are known as media. In some quarters *media* is used only to designate the electronic means of communication, primarily radio and television, but this merely confuses readers and listeners.

Journalism, a word long sufficient to represent all public communication, now is recognized mainly as referring to the print (or printed) media—newspapers, magazines, news letters, church bulletins, house publications, and in some instances, books, especially paperbacks.

A Spiritual Force

Communications is a spiritual force through its work as a popular educator, as a purveyor of facts about religion and the organized church, and as a transmitter of the ideals uttered or lived by people. The hundreds of publications concerned wholly with Christianity and its work, for example, are powerful means with which to spread the gospel. And the unchurched often are reached by secular media, through their news reports, articles, features, photographs, and programs. Each medium attempts to tell some part of the story of religion.

Although any one religion such as Christianity is not to be identified with any particular political party, social order, or form of government, the ideals of democracy in the United States and Canada depend heavily upon Christian sources. Trust in the judgment of the people is a mark of Protestantism. The thousands of congregations scattered over the continent are little democracies. They are not always perfect, to be sure, but often they work equitably.

The success of such democracies in Christendom rests upon the fullness and accuracy of information of the participants. People's opinions are no better, someone once said, than their facts. That is why totalitarian dictators are afraid to give the people all the facts. The responsibility that this situation casts upon the communications activity of print and broadcast—secular and religious—is heavy. The true believer in democracy says that if a people have all the facts the citizens' decisions can be trusted generally to be wise. From the newest cub reporter on a small daily to the person commenting via radio or television on the news before an audience of millions this responsibility must be carried seriously. Such a standard holds not merely in the realm of general information. Labor should be informed properly about management, and management should have the facts about labor. Similarly, if members of church denominations are to understand and cooperate with members of other denominations they should be informed about what the others stand for and are doing.

It is at this point, among others, that the church and the secular world meet for the public communicator. In providing facts about events that take place in the secular world, the communicator bolsters the democratic process. In providing facts about events that take place within the world of religion, the religious communicator also bolsters that process.

The Idea of Religious Vocation

In the world of religion there exists a sense of vocation or calling. Often it is applied to the ministry. But it need not be so limited, for most occupations can be vocations in a spiritual and ethical sense. It may even be that if this idea were accepted more widely the work done in the world might have a more social goal and direction than it now has. Less work that is harmful to mankind might be done.

An anonymous writer on the idea of one aspect, Christian vocation, has put it this way:

> The layman has his duties in the church in worship and stewardship. He is charged also with a task in the world outside.
>
> For most people the field of witness lies in the place where they do their daily work. The way in which they do their job or exercise their profession must be unmistakably Christian.[2]

The communicator, who most likely is a writer and therefore may be a creative artist, may not wish to be classified as a worker. But he or she is no ordinary worker, although there is nothing wrong with being an ordinary one. Dorothy L. Sayers, the British writer known most widely for her popular detective novels and somewhat less widely for her works on theology and religion, clarified the situation further by writing:

> The great primary contrast between the artist and the ordinary workers is this: the worker works to make money so that he may enjoy those things in life which are not his work and which his work can purchase for him, but the artist makes money by his work in order that he may go on working. The artist does not say: "I must work in order to live," but "I must contrive to make money so that I may live to work." For the artist there is no distinction between work and living; his work is his life, and the whole of his life—not merely the material world about him, or the colors and sounds and events that he perceives, but also all his own personality and emotions, the *whole* of his life—is the actual material of his work.[3]

Work, then, is approached in a special way by the person with a sense of vocation. The new attitude, created in the individual by this concept of vocation, gives him or her motives, aims, and goals not possessed by the person who works selfishly only. Here is an opportunity for witness. It perhaps is possible for the communicator to be of greater influence for his or her faith than the professional religious worker who may not reach so many of the unchurched and sometimes moves in a protected circle.

In Western society today, particularly in the United States, the people who hold to the idea that the religious vocation is more than professional religious work are in a minority. Religion often is compartmentalized in the lives of ordinary persons, many of whom seem to think of it as a Sunday activity to be forgotten the other days of the week. Yet, as Erma Paul Ferrari wrote about church vocation in *Careers for You:*

> If the Christian faith has any claim on our lives at all, it must be a total claim, otherwise it is only sham and make-believe. As applied to our vocational future, this means that to the Christian every job is a Christian job.[4]

The Power of Communications

Communications as a vocation, in the secular sense of being an occupation, has numerous accomplishments behind it and countless dramatic possibilities before it. In the United States, since the newspaper press passed out of the hands of politicians in the Reconstruction Years and became a business enterprise, the emphasis more and more has been on its use as a disseminator of facts, that is, news and other current information. Through publication of news and reviews of the fine and popular arts, the newspaper and the magazine industries both have broadened the everyday citizen's understanding and raised public taste in such matters, low as they still may appear in general. Newspapers, periodicals, broadcasts, and films have become popular educators more important in the lives of some persons than the formal schooling they may have received. Thousands of persons take their intimate worries to the advisers on life problems of the media, usually a poor substitute for the wiser and more sincere counsel of their religious leaders had they centered their lives in the church.

As a molder of opinion, the media are stronger in some areas of life than in others. Often they have proved more effective in local than in national politics. Charity drives owe much, usually, to the media for their success. Slum clearance campaigns, plans for new housing or public improvements, and correction of countless social ills can be credited to the various media. Journalism is limited by how far the public will let it go along educational and reform lines, for the other educational forces have not yet succeeded in bringing the public to the point where it wants education more than entertainment from the media. And the mass media, being business enterprises, cannot ignore the public's will, for if they do they will not survive unless privately subsidized.

In the effort to make itself more necessary and useful to the public, printed communications in recent decades has been attempting to discharge another function: it has sought to tell readers the meaning of events. Such explaining or interpreting usually has been the prerogative of magazines of public affairs, but with the entry of radio and television into the business of providing spot news the newspapers have added to their duty of news reporting that of news interpretation.

All these functions and accomplishments of the media

increase the possibilities of communications as a vocation for men and women whose aims in life are more than to make themselves personally secure and wealthy. In secular communications alone the opportunities are exciting and important; if to it we add the goal of living for the good of others by choosing religious communications, the possibilities are inspiring.

The Thrills of Communications

For many years communications as an occupation has been portrayed as a life of perpetual thrills, dangers, and escapades. This conventional concept for the most part is untrue. By comparison with selling shoes in a specialty shop or filing correspondence endlessly in an office, communications does offer excitement. But day by day it does not resemble the antics of television or cinema reporters or characters in a play, such as *The Front Page*.

The thrills of the communications career are to be found in the changing routine, the opportunity to know the news first and to be in on its creation, the share one has in the shaping of news stories or other copy for print or broadcast, the earning of respectable if not superstar type salaries, the chance to know many persons some of whom are makers of history, and the opportunity to be of help to one's fellows through the dissemination of facts and ideas needed as a basis for judgment and action.

Communications as a vocation has certain satisfactions for the individual that may be little different from those of carpentry, barbering, teaching, or millwork. But it is a powerful factor in society that extends the power of the individual. If that power is to be for good it must be in the hands of socially minded, dedicated persons who know how to use it and will not misuse it for selfish ends. When communications is coupled with religious idealism it is likely to transcend in social value the communications that remains a business.

For further reading about communications as a vocation:

BOOKS

Warren K. Agee, Phillip H. Ault, and Edwin Emery, *Introduction to Mass Communications*. New York: Harper & Row, 1976/Fifth Edition.

John R. Bittner, *Mass Communication: An Introduction*. Englewood Cliffs, N.J.: Prentice-Hall, 1977.

Ira H. and Beatrice O. Freeman, *Careers and Opportunities in Journalism*. New York: Dutton, 1966.

James M. Neal and Suzanne S. Brown. *Newswriting and Reporting*. Ames: Iowa State University Press, 1976.

Peter M. Sandman, David M. Rubin, and David B. Sachsman, *Media*. Englewood Cliffs, N.J.: Prentice-Hall, 1976/Second Edition.

Jeffrey Schrank, *Understanding Mass Media*. Skokie, Ill.: National Textbook, 1975.

Charles S. Steinberg, ed., *Mass Media and Communication*. New York: Hastings House, 1966.

John Tebbel, *Opportunities in Publishing Careers*. Louisville, Ky.: Vocational Guidance Manuals, 1975.

NOTES

1. James M. Neal and Suzanne S. Brown, *Newswriting and Reporting*. Ames: Iowa State University Press, 1976. pp. 4, 5.
2. From the "Report on the Witness of the Church to God's

Communications as a Vocation

Design" given at the Amsterdam meeting of the World Council of Churches.

3. From Miss Sayers' chapter, "Vocation in Work," in *A Christian Basis for the Post-War World*, a symposium published by Morehouse-Gorham, New York, 1942. Reproduced by permission.

4. Erma Paul Ferrari, *Careers for You*. Nashville, Tenn.: Abingdon-Cokesbury, 1953.

2 Communications as a Religious Vocation

In the Chapel of the Holy Grail in Disciples Divinity House at the University of Chicago in 1948, Dr. Edward Scribner Ames read a charge to James W. Carty, Jr., during an ordination service. Carty was a young Disciples minister ready to begin an unusual career. Dr. Ames said, in part:

"In ordaining you to the Christian ministry we recognize that your interest has been to equip yourself as a religious journalist. Journalists are not mentioned in the New Testament among the divinely appointed ones for the 'equipment of the saints, for the work of the ministry, for the building up of the body of Christ.' "

Then he pointed out that in the twelfth chapter of 1 Corinthians "the appointed ones" are ranked as "first apostles, second prophets, third teachers, then workers of

Communications as a Religious Vocation

miracles, then healers, helpers, administrators, speakers in various kinds of tongues."[1]

"If there had been any journalists in the apostolic age," Dr. Ames said further, "they would probably have been ranked just below the administrators! No one in that age could have imagined how many specialists would have been needed by the year 1948 for the work of the ministry. . . ."

Dr. Ames then added that "what the Apostle Paul really emphasized was that all the different gifts were to be used to promote a common purpose, and that was to build up and spread the religion of Jesus Christ. Everyone who contributes to this end is important, indeed equally important in the final estimate."

That young minister was—and still is—among the few persons ever ordained for religious communications.

Jim Carty was entering a vocation that inherently is no more religious than truck driving, mining, or the insurance business. Communications, the world over, is considered a rough-and-ready occupation, peopled largely by hard drinkers with little interest in religion. This picture never was fully accurate, however, and today is further from the truth than ever. Although the ladies and gentlemen of the press are not yet all ladies and gentlemen, the world of communications has reached heights of responsibility, dignity, and decency never attained before. It must rise higher still. Religion, nevertheless and therefore, has a place in it.

Communications' Three Possibilities

Communications clearly has possibilities as a religious vocation in at least three ways. Those persons who want to make use of them have certain choices:

1. As workers in a religious setting, such as being a staff writer for a religious newspaper or magazine issued by a church publishing house.

2. As workers in religious communications in a secular setting, such as religion editor of a secular publication.

3. As workers in secular communications who insist upon living up to their religious ideals, exemplified by a reporter who refuses to use unethical means of getting news for a radio station.

In considering further these three basic possibilities of communications as a religious vocation we should agree upon which is meant by the words *religious communications*. Together they mean *the application of the principles and techniques of communications to the world of religion.* The nature of these principles and techniques can be examined in the volumes dealing with each. (See the titles at the ends of chapters in this book.)

The person who works in religious communications in a religious setting may be a staff member of a denominational public relations office or an editor of a church publication. Or perhaps he is a missionary in another country assigned to a station (i.e., headquarters) maintained by his or her denomination and staffed mainly by other religious persons. Or he or she may do technical work connected with preparation of documentary films on religion for a broadcasting or motion picture film committee for use within the church itself.

In the second group are the persons who are church or religious news writers and editors of standard daily newspapers, magazines of many frequencies, news agencies and syndicates, or of radio and television stations. They may be employed, as well, in the religious book department of a secular book publishing firm or a church publishing house.

Typical of the third group are persons who may have nothing to do with *religious* editing, writing, reporting, or any other religious communications activity. Their duties are mainly secular, as a rule, but they take their religion seriously, and put it to work in their occupations. They attempt to conduct themselves in line with their principles, influence other journalists around them to higher moral standards (by example rather than by direct preachment), or take positions in determining policies that will bring religious ideals into use. They have active social consciences.

Communications' power for good is great under any circumstances. But its potentialities are vast when put in the hands of persons dedicated to doing their part, no matter how small, in bringing about an improved society.

Is there greater usefulness in society if communications work is done in a religious setting rather than in a secular one?

That question is a favorite of persons who come to their counselors in the church, at school, or in college, seeking aid in answering our opening question, "What shall I do with my life?" The answer to the question about the setting in which greater usefulness may lie is one of the "it all depends" kind and therefore never entirely satisfactory to someone who wishes a point-blank, categorical reply.

The answer depends partly upon the individual who raises it: his or her temperament, character, background, and skills. Partly it depends also upon the opportunity at hand and the nature of the position. And partly it depends upon who or what is to be served: is it religion, communications, the individual, or the institution?

Resolving the Issue

The issue may be resolved, perhaps, by pondering certain considerations.

In support of working within the church's own framework are these points:

1. The church itself needs trained, expert personnel. We can apply this to church communications. Scores of denominations have had to appoint ministers, religious educators, and other church persons not ordinarily trained in communications to posts as editors and managers of their publications and to public relations as well as broadcasting and film offices. Sometimes the decision has served as an expedient to satisfy some internal political situation. It may be the consequence of a denominational merger, in which all factions uniting must be given equal representation in communications. Sometimes—and far more often now than in the past—the decision springs from lack of trained people within the denomination. Thus men and women who equip themselves to do communications tasks are meeting a vocational need that almost always has been difficult to meet properly.

2. Most persons work better in a sympathetic, understanding atmosphere than in one that is indifferent to the individual and remains detached. Instead of being stimulated by impartiality, unconcern, or opposition they are discouraged. But they can do extraordinary work—or at

least are more likely to do it—when surrounded by persons of similar aims and ideals. This matter is psychological and temperamental.

An instance at the student level is a young man whom we shall call Mark Submarro, who came to the United States on a church scholarship to study religious journalism. The first university he attended had no particular interest in such journalism. His teachers, though friendly and technically excellent, were neither informed about that aspect of communications nor concerned about the possibilities for Mark in work which would utilize his religious ideals in his vocation. Feeling himself an outsider, receiving no encouragement, and receiving no guidance, he did only passably in his studies. Then, hearing of another institution which had great interest in religious communications, he transferred. Mark worked more diligently than ever before in his life, winning the respect of his teachers for his carefully prepared term papers, his quick grasp of techniques, and his dependability and sincere attitude. He later returned to his own country to become, in time, editor of a leading religious periodical.

3. The worker in the religious setting can go more deeply into the ideas he wishes to advance through communications, for his is a religiously well-informed audience. At least it is by comparison with the degree of religious enlightenment of the general public. Thus he can support the cause of religious knowledge and understanding. At the same time he—these days it may just as well be a she—can do all this through communications work, which is an entirely different way of doing so from any other available to him—or her.

In the Secular World

What of the religious person working in secular communications with a relationship to religion?

1. The chance to reach the unchurched is far greater, since secular publications, broadcasts, and films are seen and heard by persons with many different views and attitudes toward religion. In other words, the evangelistic opportunity is far greater here.

The strictly secular press, for example, is far more widely and intensely read than is the religious. Only a few religious publications in the United States ever have reached one million circulation; a few which are practically given away claim from two to thirty million but there is no evidence that any particular number are read. One secular magazine, *Reader's Digest*, has a paid circulation of thirty million throughout the world but provides evidence of substantial readership. It is no exaggeration to say that one article on religion in that pocket-sized monthly has more influence on more persons in general than almost any one hundred articles in the rest of the church press that same month. This result is achieved purely by sheer exposure to millions of readers around the world of any single piece of writing in that magazine.

2. The influence also is upon the publication or other medium itself, and thus an indirect influence of great significance upon readers, listeners, and viewers. Staff members who apply their religion have influenced those persons responsible for newspapers, magazines, the output of radio and television stations, and other media to adopt policies that conform to religious ideals.

When Jim Carty joined the staff of the *Sun* in Yukon,

Oklahoma, for instance, the editor printed a story about him. Over it he put: "Notice—Please Don't Use Cuss Words Around Yukon *Sun's* New 'Calf Editor.' " During a religious journalism seminar conducted by the Nashville *Tennessean*, a large daily Jim joined later to become religious news editor, the editor of the paper told a large audience that the city room of the paper became a much better place because of Jim's presence. On other publications the existence of practicing religious people helps to determine such policies as the refusal of liquor advertising, insistence upon publication of news that might displease advertisers, and use of pictures that do not violate good taste, and—what may really be far more vital—supporting views on public affairs consistent with the highest ideals of the church.

If possible, newcomers to religious communications should practice it inside as well as outside the world of professional religion itself. Then they may better understand the various problems and finally settle down to a kind of work which has proved itself the more satisfactory for realizing their abilities and making greater use of their aptitudes.

The Religious Irreligionists

If the reader of these words has pondered the viewpoints explained thus far, he or she is likely to think that the only really useful communicator is the one who, directly and consciously, follows religious principles. This implication is not intended. Most of us derive our best moral attitudes from religion, but not always directly. In fact, some of the most ardent fighters for the good causes are disdainful of religion, but usually they were influenced by early reading, parental attitudes, or religious colleagues. They have been touched, somehow, by religious ideals. The work of these religious irreligionists is by no means, however, as consistently socially useful or valuable as that of the conscientiously religious person.

Dick Wheately (not his real name), for example, never went to church, took no part in active religious life, and was indifferent to his wife's interest in the church and enrollment of their small son in church school. This young editor nevertheless was daily becoming more and more disgusted with the unethical practices in his magazine office. Circulation figures were falsified; professional standards were low (deadlines missed often, copy sloppily edited, coverage of subjects was superficial). Dick gave up the job without assurance of another because he did not want to support or seem to support his publication's policies any longer, for he did not believe in them. He never admitted that his attitude sprang from religious idealism, but he did say that some of his former associates had implanted certain ideals before he joined this particular magazine staff. It turned out that those associates were church people.

But the shoddy practices at Dick's office continued; unless the religious irreligionist achieves major changes he adjusts only his own conscience and does not improve the situation to which he objected.

Just as it is easier to be a good church person by going to church, so it is easier to live religiously in a religious setting or by doing a religious job in a secular setting. But the apparently nonreligious persons—or those who so consider themselves—also are to be honored for their unconscious championing of religious ideals. They are deprived, nevertheless, of the utmost satisfaction in what they are doing. They are not so likely to be happy in their work as the people in communications work committed to religion. Annie Ward Byrd, at one time an editor for the Baptist Sunday School Board, pointed up the difference when she wrote:

> What kinds of people make the best religious journalists and are happiest in the job?
> First of all, the person has to believe in the message he is trying to propagate. A religious journalist must have a deep religious faith. . . .
> Furthermore, he must feel a sense of commitment to the task of sharing the good news of God's love with others. In short, he must love God and people, too.[2]

Jim Carty's Career

Jim Carty, part of whose career story has been told already, as a religious person chose to work in the secular world of communications. In his ordination statement he said, after tracing the source of his views:

> Either a minister should work for the creation of a vital new Christian life, or he should point out to his people the existence of Christian life in other localities, in other forms of expression so that they can take faith that they are not alone, and second can align themselves with these other movements and men. My own interest in religious journalism would seem to add to the second-named function. By describing the happenings of Christian vitalities everywhere I may, in a small way, be saying to Christians: Take heart, Christianity does exist somewhere. And if your own environment temporarily is too tough for Christianity, join with these vitalities in other communities.

What was the background of the man who reached that decision?

A Missourian, Jim went to grade and high schools in that state. From Culver-Stockton College at Canton, Missouri, he earned his BA, and then was awarded a 3-year scholarship at the University of Chicago to obtain his divinity degree. After being ordained a religious journalist his first opportunity to put his ambition to work came from Pastor W. H. Alexander of Oklahoma City. Jim was made director of public relations, youth work, and education at the First Christian Church. Realizing that he needed more of both schooling and journalistic experience, he enrolled at the University of Oklahoma for graduate study in education, sociology, and psychology and also found himself a job on the *Daily Oklahoman*.

This practical work made Jim realize, as he later put it, that he "was too abstract a writer; that was the trouble with theological seminary." He shifted to the *Daily Whig-Herald* at Quincy, Illinois, when retrenchment hit the *Oklahoman*. At Quincy he handled general assignments but also had some church news to write. Soon he moved to the Yukon *Sun*, whose welcome we already have recorded earlier in this chapter. Although there was more church news to the job, Carty knew that he needed still more formal training, so he enrolled in the Medill School of Journalism at Northwestern University. He received his master's degree in journalism there.

From Illinois he went to Tennessee, to Nashville's large daily, the *Tennessean*, where the practice has been to put people who wish to be specialists through some standard assignments first. Jim still cannot forget the way

Professor James W. Carty, Jr., first at right, and E. C. Makunike, second left, discuss photojournalism with two students from African schools at the Africa Literature Centre in Zambia. Mr. Makunike, director of the Centre, holds a journalism degree from an American university.

the detectives and policemen down at the station watched their language when he walked in. "We have to be careful when the Reverend is around," they said. Then he was assigned to the religious newsbeat.

Carty covered that news specialty for ten years before leaving daily journalism to become professor of journalism and director of public relations and publications at Bethany College, Bethany, West Virginia. His teaching career has by no means ended his writing activities. He continues to contribute dozens of articles annually to numerous religious and secular newspapers and magazines. His books include *Advertising the Local Church, Communicating with God,* and *The Gresham Years.* He is coauthor of *Relaciones Publicas,* a volume in Spanish on public relations.

During summers and leaves of absence since the early 1960s, he has had more than a dozen overseas assignments. He has been a Fulbright lecturer in Nicaragua, where he taught communications for a year, having learned Spanish, has taught in Egypt and Tanzania, and has written literacy materials for use in a Christian adult literacy program in East Africa. He has lectured in Zambia, written interviews for religious publications in South Africa and Rhodesia in recent years, and has taught religious communications courses in Puerto Rico. This work has brought him awards from various religious and secular communications organizations, and invitations to teach at other universities and colleges, some of which he has done at Ohio and West Virginia universities.

Other Communicators of Religion

Working quietly, as has Jim Carty, are dozens of other men and women active in some area of religious communications through the various media. Some of those who stood out in the past or are influential today include Paul Hutchinson, G. Elson Ruff, Elsie Culver, Harold Fey, Robert Hoyt, Helen E. Baker, George Walker Buckner, Jr., Robert J. Cadigan, Paul Eby, Henry L. Mc-

Corkle, Carl F. H. Henry, Erwin H. Canham, Alfred M. Klausler, William B. Lipphard, Janette Harrington, Kenneth Wilson, and Louise Moseley. All were or are active in publications or public relations work. Charles Schmitz and Everett Parker are closely identified with radio and television. Among the information specialists the prominent names include Ralph Stoody, Stanley Stuber, Arthur West, W.C. Fields, Erik Modean, and Fletcher Coates. The writers of religious news for secular publications whose names stand out are Willmar Thorkelson, James Supple, George Dugan, Ora Spaid, John Cogley, Harrison W. Fry, Margaret A. Vance, Caspar Nannes, David A. Runge, and others whose biographies appear in the chapter related to such communications. Many more names of merit could be added.

A few of these persons were assisted in achieving their vocational and religious goals by being trained in both religion and communications, but most had only one or the other, and some had neither. In recent years a greater premium has been put upon communications training. Parallel with the moral improvement in the communications world, as already noted, has been a much slower but still sure process: the professionalizing of the world of religious communications. There was a time when the new editor of a church magazine was almost certain to be a complete stranger to the workings of the press or broadcasting: a superannuated pastor, a successful preacher, or a board executive with promotional ability. And almost always the editor was a man; that, too, is changing. Rarely was the journalist given preference. (See the separate survey report on training in Chapter 10.)

Largely this misfitting occurred because the combination of religious worker and communicator was rare. The appointing body naturally had to select someone familiar with the denomination, acquainted with its history and policies, and known to its constituency. The arts of writing and editing might not be his, but the hope was that they would be acquired, somehow (perhaps by osmosis), that nobody would know the difference, or some badly paid assistant would provide the techniques then held in such low esteem.

Demands Become Greater

As secular communications improved, awakened readers made greater demands upon the religious communicators. As education for the field developed, more and more young people who took seriously both their religion and their profession began calling at and writing to religious publication houses and public relations offices seeking work. As religious publications have had to meet the competition for the leisure time of citizens from better secular print journalism, radio, television, films, and spectator sports as well, their publishers have given more thought to their practices in engaging personnel. And they are adding such persons to their staffs more often. (See the boxed reports in Chapter 10.)

To be sure, the extent to which communications is being used as a religious vocation still is small by comparison with the use of medicine and education, especially in missionary enterprises. No longer is it a novelty to find students in theological seminaries, university schools and departments of journalism or communications, and among communications majors in arts college who plan to enter some phase of religious communications. For the Christians among them it is an opportunity to "build up and spread the religion of Jesus Christ." And for those of other faiths it is a chance to inform the world of their beliefs and standards, be they Jews, Hindus, Muslims, or of other North American religious minorities.

This opportunity is a clue to the difference between a secular and a religious vocation. The chief distinction may be in the goals for the individual. The aim or purpose in life of the person concerned affects his or her daily conduct and long-range decisions. There also are the aims of the occupation itself. Five tests of an occupation to determine if it is Christian have been noted by the Interboard Committee on Christian Vocations: "It must meet real human need, be morally constructive and helpful, call for the full use of one's talents, build fellowship, and evoke from the workers a conviction that God calls one to serve."

Communications does not fulfill such aims automatically or involuntarily. Religious communications is more likely to do so, since often that is its intention.

For further reading about communications as a religious vocation and on communications as a career in general:

BOOKS

Careers in Canadian Magazines. Toronto: Magazine Association of Canada, 1976.

Lyman Abbot, *Reminiscences.* Boston: Houghton Mifflin, 1915.

Richard Terrill Baker, *The Christian as a Journalist*. New York: Association Press, 1961.

Harry C. Broome, Jr., *Opportunities in Advertising Careers*. Louisville, Ky.: Vocational Guidance Manuals, 1976.

Ira V. Brown, *Lyman Abbott*. Cambridge, Mass.: Harvard University Press, 1953.

John Cogley, *A. Canterbury Tale: Experiences and Reflections, 1916-1976*. New York: Seabury Press, 1976.

Ira H. and Beatrice O. Freeman, *Careers and Opportunities in Journalism*. New York: 1966.

Margaret Harmon, *Working with Words: Careers for Writers*. Philadelphia: Westminster, 1977.

John A. Hostetler, *God Uses Ink*. Scottdale, Pa.: Herald Press, 1958.

William B. Lipphard, *Fifty Years an Editor*. Valley Forge, Pa.: Judson Press, 1963.

Erwin L. McDonald, *Across the Editor's Desk*. Nashville, Tenn.: Broadman Press, 1966.

E. C. Routh, *Adventures in Christian Journalism*. Nashville, Tenn.: Broadman Press, 1951.

Clarence O. Schlaver, ed., *Careers in Journalism. The Quill*, November, 1970. Vol. 58, No. 11.

James E. Sellers, *The Outsider and the Word of God*. New York: Abingdon Press, 1961.

M. L. Stein, *Your Career in Journalism*. New York: Messner, 1965.

W. Bertrand Stevens, *Editor's Quest*. New York: Morehouse-Gorham, 1940.

John Tebbel, *Opportunities in Publishing Careers*. Louisville, Ky.: Vocational Guidance Manuals, 1975.

Irwin St. John Tucker, *Out of the Hell-Box*. New York:

Morehouse-Gorham, 1945.

F. Deaville Walker, *William Carey*. Chicago: Moody Press, 1951.

Ellrose D. Zook, *Wanted: Christian Journalists*. Scottdale, Pa.: *Youth's Christian Companion* reprint of a series, 1960.

ARTICLES

Gregory Baum, "Toward the Seventies: Issues in Religious Journalism." *The Word at Work*, April 1969, quarterly of the World Literacy and Christian Literature. Also in *Copy Log*, January 1969, publication of the Associated Church Press.

Phillip W. Butler, "Christian Radio and TV." *Interlit*, June 1976.

"1975 Annual Report Issue." *Interlit*, March 1976.

"Communications Issue." *Motive*, March 1957.

Joseph Wood Krutch, "Man Is More Than a Statistic." *Saturday Review*, May 21, 1966.

Mike LeFan, "Religious Journalism: Is That the Job for You?" *Reachout*, December 2, 1973.

"We Hold These Truths—Magnificent Task." Editorial, *The Youth's Instructor*, November 28, 1967.

"What's Behind Christian Films?" A symposium. *Interlit*, June 1976.

NOTES

1. 1 Corinthians 12:27, Revised Standard Version, Thomas Nelson & Sons, New York, 1946 and 1952.
2. From a pamphlet, *Religious Journalism*, published by the Southern Baptist Convention, Nashville, Tenn.

3 The Job Situation

The opportunities and working conditions of religious communications, as they do in many other occupations, change from time to time. As the economy alters, as the political situation changes, and as the attitudes of the people—including those in the churches—shift, the job situation is affected.

During most of its existence, the religious communications field has been one of relatively low pay but high opportunity to be of service through the various media. Working conditions often have been mediocre in quality but the human relations have been exceptional. The religious media usually have welcomed newcomers and have served as training grounds as well as careers in themselves.

How one evaluates a career in any field depends upon

The Job Situation 45

one's values. If the primary purpose is to make and accumulate money, the occupation of religious communicator may just as well be forgotten at once. It is not intended to be a moneymaking vocation on a large scale anymore than is the ministry or missionary service.

To be sure, the laborer is worthy of his hire. Serious inequities have existed in the field and probably always will, as in every occupation. The dilemma of the managers of church-related media is that most of them want to pay adequate salaries and in good times do so, but when recession and depression hit the world or the nation they cannot do as well as they wish. On the contrary, some of them must cease operations or fail to expand and improve their enterprises. They are caught in the sickness of the economic order of which their establishments are only one part.

An earlier edition of this book began this chapter with evidence that in the 1950s and 1960s the demand for communications personnel by the world of religion was surprisingly high. Publications and related communications activities, particularly public relations, were expanding and needed more trained persons for staff. Then economic distress struck the communications business generally as a result of widespread economic malaise, and the wing concerned with religion felt the effects. The demand for workers naturally decreased.

While now a smaller field than a decade ago, it is by no means closed. Also, technological changes are affecting it in such a way that new personnel will be needed. The publications need copy, so writers are wanted. The editors and publishers need staff people alert to the social and religious trends of the day. (See comments in the separate survey report in this chapter.)

It is a characteristic of truly religious persons that they enter a field of work because they are needed. It is like them to put up with less than ideal wages and working conditions, if necessary, for the joy of being of service, for the chance to help accomplish what is to be done to help mankind. That attitude is a precious one, and should not be abused or taken advantage of, as a few of the entrepreneurs of religious communications sometimes do.

And today, in the last quarter of the 20th century, the need for religious communications is as great as ever. That need stems from the appalling conditions in which mankind finds itself. If religion is to fulfill its function (and here one must assume that all religions have a high social purpose but admit that some may fall short of that purpose) there must be solutions to the overwhelming problems facing the beings who live on this planet.

A glance at any general newspapers or a half hour of listening to a thorough newscast can reveal a part of the situation in a troubled and confused world. After a week of listening, viewing, and reading one realizes that humanity is beset by foundering governments; problems resulting from overpopulation and underproduction; need for massive campaigns to overcome various diseases; malnutrition affecting millions; increasing breakdown of once well-established moral codes; trembling in the institution of marriage; inadequate housing and sanitation for many millions of the world's inhabitants; mounting crime statistics; continued warring between political groups identified as Christians, Muslims, and Jews; and steady increases in the number of nations being ruled by civilian autocrats and military dictators. These are just some of the enormous problems in the world today.

To be sure, mainly bad news dominates the media, since bad news, fortunately, is the exception rather than the rule. Yet the quantity of such news certainly is great enough to offer the religious communicator challenges sufficient to last a lifetime. The call to the mission of communications rings clear.

The problem of converting the desire to help into a chance to work never has been easy for the dedicated writer, editor, or other communications worker. The field of religious communications has always been relatively small. Only about one in twenty-five publications in the United States, for example, is devoted to religion, and usually it has a small circulation. The radio stations concerned basically with religion are only a handful. Only major newspapers, newsmagazines, news services, and broadcasting chains employ specialists on religion. Certain auxiliary services—publicity and public relations, printing, and advertising—use such specialists, but not in high numbers. The indirect opportunities of serving while in the secular field now are more limited than during the affluent 1950s and 1960s but precisely what they amount to has not been calculated.

Openings do exist in all these areas and will continue to exist. Personnel changes—death takes some, new jobs attract others, modest expansion occurs here and there, overseas possibilities still are strong, free-lancing is feasible for those gifted as writers, artists, and photographers. Encouraging views appear in the survey reports that are a part of this chapter and Chapter 10.

The procedures to be used in connecting the ambition with the job are discussed in the final chapter. The need for the religious communicator is great still.

Training Is Appreciated

Whatever the size of the demand, it is characterized by appreciation for trained applicants. The growing preference for them is explained readily.

Education and training for journalism began soon after the turn of the present century. Gradually such preparation was launched later to cover all media. As more college-trained persons entered communications they in turn, once they became hirers and firers, tended to engage trained persons, often from their own colleges and universities. Furthermore, communications itself has become more complex and efficient than in its early years. Greater talent, ability, and specialized knowledge are demanded of applicants; training helps to find and select the most competent personnel in a computer age. Also, the power and the importance of the printed word and broadcast scene or picture are greater than ever in this interrelated world, as is shown by the increase in numbers of certain types of publications and the high circulations of virtually all established ones. Added to these are the existence of publicity and public relations offices and religious radio and television as well as film positions.

Career seekers should be informed about the institutions they hope to join and, in particular, what kinds of positions might be held. Titles do not necessarily indicate duties and responsibilities, but at least they are a clue to the area of work that might be done.

Publishing Houses

In general, religious publishing firms are organized like any others that produce magazines, newspapers, books, leaflets, and similar literature. Their motives are different, for financial profit ordinarily is not supposed to be the main objective. They aim to promote religious beliefs held by the sponsoring body, to serve readers by helping them to live better lives, and to stimulate religious loyalty and action.

The larger religious publications houses engage practically all the usual personnel for such work. Common titles are:

Editorial department—editor-in-chief, executive editor, managing editor, art editor, production editor, news editor, senior editor, associate editor, assistant editor, and editorial assistant in more or less descending order of responsibility. Not all firms use these titles or all these titles.

Advertising department—manager or director, space salesman, copywriter, layout chief, production assistant, researcher. Most religious publications leave such work to agencies or companies hired to do it for a number of magazine, newspaper, or book publishers.

Circulation department—manager or director, salesman, mailing room foreman, circulation clerk. Here again some publications find it less expensive to hire professional firms to do circulation work, rather than maintain a staff to do it.

Promotion department—manager or director, artist, publicity writer, photographer. Outside firms are likely to be used by most publishers for this service, but a church organization which produces considerable literature can keep a staff of its own busy at promotion.

Business department—manager, comptroller, accountant, secretary, statistician, computer division manager.

Production department—manager, assistant or deputy manager, engraving and other subdivision heads, including computer operations, foremen, machinists, and other workers in printing. This department exists only if the publishing office has a large enough volume to operate its own plant, which is true of a number of major denominations.

In all these departments are secretaries, clerks, and stenographers from whose ranks executives sometimes rise.

Religious news agencies and feature syndicates number only about a dozen in the United States. Around two dozen more firms, secular in their activities, include some religious materials in their services. Few opportunities exist, therefore, on the staffs of these organizations. Writing, editing, processing, and selling of the output, which consists of news stories, features, fiction, cartoons, photographs, and educational materials particularly related to the Bible, are work done by a few persons.

Public Relations Offices

Church public relations, publicity, and information offices are another matter. This area is closely related to standard religious communications, for it uses all the techniques employed to produce publications and broadcasts of every nature. It has been expanding in the past three decades as denominational groups, ecumenical organizations, and other religious bodies have realized that they must put their stories before the publics they

The Job Situation

wish to reach by using all media of communications when possible. To do so requires planning, knowledge of those media, and the ability to use the techniques of mass communications effectively.

Several dozen large Christian denominations and a few Jewish bodies maintain publicity or public relations offices, as do some of the smaller ones. So do the World Council of Churches, the National Council of Churches, and scores of less widely known organizations of religion. Institutions and boards within denominations also do so. All depend heavily upon persons with communications experience and training. They employ administrative personnel, news and feature writers, photographers, artists, editors, and editorial or publicity assistants. Sometimes specialized outside firms are engaged to do such work; they need on their staffs persons of religious background and professional ability as well.

Managers of small offices expect their staff members to combine some of these skills. The head of a branch or regional office would need to write news and feature releases for newspapers, magazines, newsletters, and broadcasting companies, in the sense that such copy is aimed at those media with the hope that it will be used. Such an executive himself or herself might prepare articles; take pictures or at least direct a photographer; prepare copy for leaflets, booklets, brochures, and other promotional literature; and edit all this copy and see it through production stages. He or she also spends time arranging for radio and television appearances of newsmakers in the group served. The head or an aide is called upon to speak in public and to advise others in need of publicity or public relations service.

Secular publications and radio-television stations that employ staff to handle their religious materials naturally need fewer personnel for this purpose than do religious agencies. Daily newspapers in the United States number around 1,780; weeklies, about 8,000; magazines of all types and frequencies, 20,000; news agencies and syndicates, 1,000. The dailies employ about 700 persons as church or religion news writers, but most of them are not full time on the specialty. Only the largest news-gathering agencies, the Associated Press and United Press International, have religion news writers and editors full time. Even the small daily newspapers combine the church or religious news reporters' work with some other responsibility. Occasionally a secular publicity concern handles religious accounts in sufficient number to add temporarily a staffer who specializes in religious publicity. Only the larger radio and television networks engage full-time religious specialists.

Radio and Television Stations

By comparison with the total number of radio and television stations in operation, those dedicated to religion are only a handful. Four networks own three dozen between them but have about 2,500 affiliates for radio broadcasts. These networks have more than 600 primary affiliated TV stations as well. The total number of radio stations in the United States is about 4,500 FM and around 3,500 AM; the FM stations are divided about three to one commercial as against educational. The domination of commercial stations holds as well in television. Of the approximately 600 VHF stations about 100 are education and more than 500 commercial. The ratio

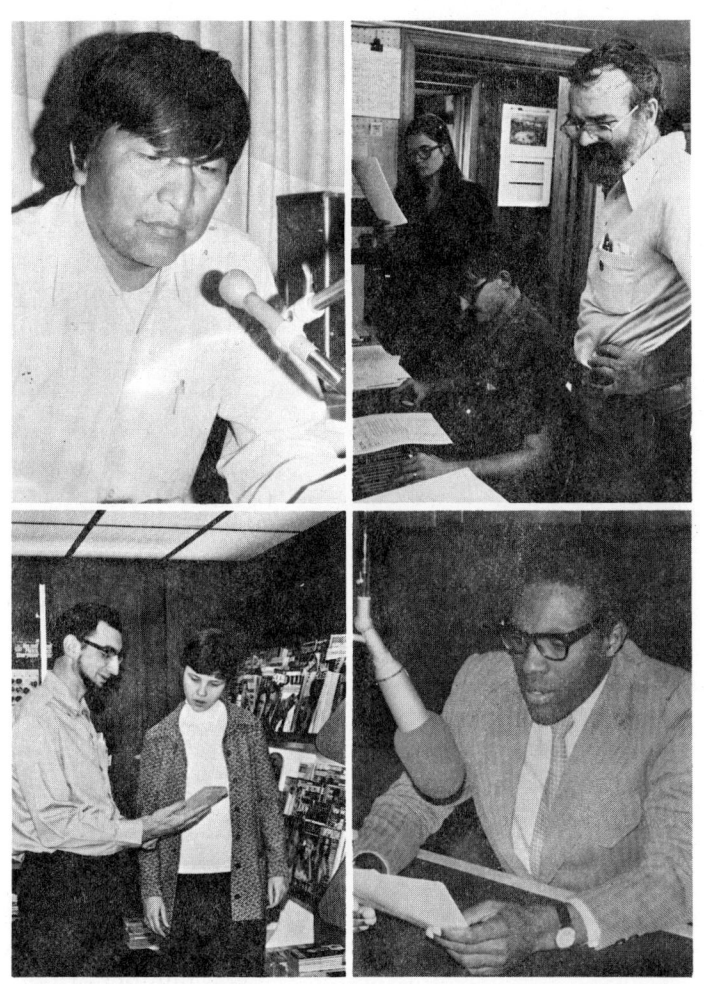

These four photographs represent the work of Mennonite Broadcasts, Inc., in Harrisonburg, Virginia. Clockwise beginning at upper left: Peter Burbank of Chinle, Arizona, recording a message for the Navajo Gospel Hour; *Melodie Miller Davis, staff writer, Larry Heatwole, studio manager and engineer, and James G. Fairfield, creative consultant, record voice talent for a series of radio spots for youth; Samuel Walters, of Kingston, Jamaica, a speaker on the English language program,* The Way to Life, *released to the Caribbean; and Simon Schrock, supervisor of Choice Books of Northern Virginia, discussing sales with the assistant bookshop manager of Dulles Airport, Washington.*

is closer in the UHF category, with 196 of them commercial and 147 education.

Religious radio and television have an important place within secular broadcasting, which provides far more opportunities for persons able to create materials for use in those media than do the few stations of either medium devoted entirely to religion. The organization of these stations in general is the same whatever the material being broadcast except that the religious stations, being among the smallest, have few persons on their staffs.

Although broadcasting is a big field it does not employ as large a number of persons as might be expected with its enormous outreach. Since many of its operations are mechanical and electronic, it needs less personnel. And of its personnel, few are related to communications in the sense the word is used in this book. The news and feature staffs of most stations are a small part of the total of persons employed, for many of the others are technicians, salespersons, and managers. A small city radio station, which might be comparable to the largest run by religionists, generally has about one fifth the number of full-time writers as the same community's daily newspaper.

When such stations hire persons with communications training they are engaged as reporters, script editors, announcers, and assignment editors, the latter functioning as a city editor does on a newspaper. Camera men and women often outnumber the editorial personnel because the electronic media depend upon local, national, and international news services and sources provided by network affiliations for program materials of a journalistic nature.

The Job Situation

Religious Books

All books are communications media, although most of them are not journalism. More and more, however, the book world operates in a journalistic manner. Paperbacks can be produced in a matter of weeks. They are distributed on newsstands much as if they were magazines or newspapers. Many of the editorial and production skills used by journalists are employed as well in book publishing offices, although the timing may be different and the need for precision greater and more possible, since pressure is less.

Added to the standard journalistic publishing firms already examined as making use of communications workers should be the more than one hundred firms that issue books about religion. Between them these houses edit and publish books on many aspects of religion in all faiths, curriculum materials, and other nonjournalistic reading matter, such as art materials for use in church school classes.

Books about religion are numerically among the leaders annually in the United States. Many religious firms are also entering general book publishing, issuing volumes with no direct connection with religion, at least in the conventional sense. This trend opens opportunities to writers not interested in or capable of producing theological works and other kinds of standard religious books; editorial and salespeople also are benefited.

Training for the book publishing field is restricted to an occasional evening course in a metropolitan university, intended for new employees in the field or for those seeking positions as beginners. Communications education is a valuable form of preparation proved by the fact that graduates of schools and departments of journalism and communications are engaged in book publishing, including religious.

Religious book houses are departmentalized as are other publishing ventures, with editorial, art and graphics, sales and advertising, and promotion and publicity divisions. An administrative division oversees the lot; usually a board representing the denomination, if the firm is owned by such a body, controls budget and other business matters.

Photographers and Artists

Photography is so much a technique and an art that its dedication to the uses of religion is not a common concept, as are other types of communications. Yet the proficient camera expert whose purposes are social deserves honor just as does the writer who puts his or her skill at the service of religion.

Photography and artwork are mentioned here and there in this book in noting what editors do on the job, what writers need to submit with their written copy, and what broadcasting companies require for their operations. But the service of the photographer should not be assumed. Anyone skilled with a camera has an important place in religious communications, more so than ever before, as does the artist who can draw sketches for book jackets, paint illustrations for children's and adult literature, and prepare page layouts.

As with the writer, editor, or advertising worker, photographers and other artists can serve their religious faith in secular as well as directly religious work. The larger church publishing houses employ artists full time.

Religious publications use photographs and artwork and generally pay for them on a free-lance basis. Religious broadcasters need both still and motion picture camera artists as well as illustrators and other graphic artists.

Art and photography are valuable specialties which can be put to good use in many areas of religious communications.

The Story Papers

Hundreds of persons are on the staffs of what commonly are called "the story papers." Many hundreds more write short stories, articles, and poems or draw or take pictures for them, yet they receive little recognition as being part of religious communications.

Usually story papers are small-size publications distributed at church schools to the various age groups, mainly children and youth. They have such names as *Reachout, Accent on Youth, Roadrunner,* and *Teens Today*. Probably many a reader of this book read and was influenced by them in his or her early years. Usually their contents reflect strong religious motives, but their concept of the function of the church has been broadening.

Often these papers and magazines are starting places for new staff members as well as contributors. Young or new writers wishing to use religion as a subject should study them, try to write for them, and strive to find places on their editorial mastheads. Competition for work on them is far less keen than it is for positions on the more widely promoted publications for adults in the churches. And much can be learned from the editors of the best of them. Sometimes these publications are too elaborate physically to be called merely "papers." They are combined, in some instances, with lesson materials and serve valuable educational purposes. Their receptiveness to writers is extraordinary.

The Religious Communicator as Educator

Communicators cannot help being educators. Publications and broadcasts, whether designed as textbooks or educational guides, can be and often are educational tools, for they impart knowledge, create opinions, and help develop the power to think. Religious communications and communicators are no exception.

One area associated with religious communications, that known as curriculum writing, is directly educational. These materials are graded lessons for use in church school classes. Experienced writers on religion have testified that preparing these educational articles or books is one of the most difficult tasks they ever have performed. This may explain why the demand for acceptable copy is so great and the payment so much higher than for most other kinds of writing in the religious field.

Writers of these materials must know teaching methods, write clearly and attractively, and understand the vocabulary, mind-set, and interests of the special group of readers at whom the writing is aimed. They also are expected to conform to the position of their church on various theological and social issues and yet encourage free discussion, provide information, and provoke thought. Only a portion of such writing is journalistic; perhaps if more of it were so the lesson materials might be still more widely and intensively used than at present.

Here is another opportunity, then, for free-lancers as

well as would-be staff members of church publishing houses and divisions of church school literature.

Other Areas

Although relatively small, missionary communications overseas is far more significant than the numbers of persons engaged in it. It is a different form of evangelism than that practiced by the traditional missionary of the nineteenth century. Missionary communicators can be linked with medical missionaries because they manifest their faith by their deeds rather than directly by their words.

Also, there are opportunities to teach religious communications and the much larger but rarely full-time occupation of being a free-lance writer on religion. These opportunities are explained in more detail in succeeding chapters, with examples of the careers of persons engaged in such activities.

The Charges Against Communications

Mass communications as a business are frequently under fire from critics. If the charges are merited, the religionists who work in secular situations have the opportunity to improve conditions. They must not miss the chance to stand for their principles and exercise their influence, even if it be in a limited way.

What are some of the major charges against American secular communications? Here are some echoes of the criticisms by the Commission on Freedom of the Press and other critics of the past three decades. The mass media, it has been declared repeatedly, have become businesses lacking courage, heart, or soul. The newspapers waste space on trivia, neglect important international news for sensational domestic stories, and clutter up their pages with astrology columns, crossword puzzles, yards of comic strips, and other entertainment material. They are, the charges go, at the beck and call of their advertisers, and they help too little to bring about reforms in social practices and in the political world.

American magazines, according to the judges of the media, print too many pieces of silly fiction, innocuous articles, and harmful advertising based upon fear and the keeping-up-with-the-Jones' appeals. They promote intoxicating liquors and cancer-inducing tobacco products as well as expensive luxury items that citizens should not be tempted to buy. They pamper their readers rather than showing an interest in improving conditions for mankind, such as helping to rid the world of war, poverty, illiteracy, hunger, and ill health. Similar accusations are made against radio, television, and the film industry; these businesses are blamed for the increases in violence in daily life, the decay of the institution of marriage, and the exploitation of sex.

This book is not the place to evaluate such charges, but some of the volumes that do are listed at the end of this chapter; they explore the situation in depth.

To whatever extent the charges are true, however, religious communicators, whatever their faith, have the opportunity to help bring about improvement. On the staffs of dailies, as editorial writers, they may urge honest facing of community issues rather than evasiveness. They can give harassed publishers encouragement and support. On the staffs of secular magazines they can assign and welcome articles that tackle important ideas and, of course, give attention to religion. In the early days of American communications, newspapers and magazines allotted far more space to religion than they now do. Why? Because the American people as a whole, including editors and publishers, then were more actively re-

The General Situation in Religious Communications

Twenty-eight directors of communications, public relations, publicity, or public information and heads of organization in religious communications were asked, late in 1976, the question: "How would you characterize the job situation in general in religious communications at this time?" Twenty-three responded. Below are some of the replies. The result of the survey shows that thirteen are optimistic about the present situation, four were not, and six gave mixed answers.

The job situation in religious communications in this period is a wide open field. The climate is apparently very healthy for pursuit in the field . . . as perhaps never before.
—*Raymond J. Lewis*, director Promotion and Public Relations, American Baptist Association.

The job situation in the so-called "main line" churches is at about the same level as in the past, although most of these churches have been gaining in membership and financial support after a lean and depressing decade.
—*John C. Goodbody*, Executive for Communication, Executive Council of the Episcopal Church.

Evangelical publishing is enjoying an upswing. . . . We have the largest-ever membership in EPA now.
—*Richard G. Champion*, President, Evangelical Press Association, Managing Editor, The Pentecostal Evangel.

I characterize the job situation in general . . . as a fertile field for young aspirants. Many denominations are just now beginning to explore the possibilities in media for Christian education and other

ligious, at least in the conventional ways. As more and more religious-minded persons find important places on the staffs of present-day publications and broadcasting stations, religious facts and ideas will have more chances to be heard, read, and seen.

Another Great Opportunity

Within religious communications itself reforms also

---

religious communications. ... I believe there will be an increasing demand ... in the near future.
—*Paul G. Settle*, Coordinator, Committee for Christian Education and Publications, Presbyterian Church in America.

Generally, we foresee an acceleration in job opportunities ... as churches more and more use the electronic media particularly in telling their messages.
—*Wendell J. Ashton*, Managing Director, Public Communications Department, The Church of Jesus Christ of Latter-day Saints.

In the field of denominational communications, job opportunities are extremely limited.
—*William T. McKee*, Executive Secretary, American Baptist Churches U.S.A.

Many denominations are searching for the right people and are doing their utmost to recruit and develop personnel wherever possible.
—*Colonel George Nelting*, National Chief Secretary, The Salvation Army.

The job situation in general in religious communications is stable at this time. Several denominations have cut back in communications' staff, but I believe the retrenchment has now ceased and that communications will continue to be seen as a vital force in the life of a denomination.
—*Nelson Price*, Director, Public Media Division, United Methodist Church.

I think the job situation is improving. Certainly we are

are needed: publishing standards should be higher, salaries should be more in line with the cost of living, and greater courage should be exhibited by those in charge of the religious media. Thus there are great opportunities of which religious writers, editors, advertising experts, or other workers can avail themselves. Most religious publications were hampered by lack of money and know-how for many years. Only recently have many of them finding this true in our own denomination, although there is still much room for improvement.

—*M. Carol Hetzell*, Director, Department of Communication, General Conference of Seventh-day Adventists.

Religion will continue to be preeminently a communications cause.... Unquestionably, the churches and synagogues and their institutions and agencies will be looking for more and more communications talent as we move into the future.

—*Wilmer C. Fields*, Assistant to the Executive Secretary, Director of Public Relations, Southern Baptist Convention.

At this point in the history of publication in many so-called main line denominations ... the job situation is not so good. However, there are always openings for one reason or another and qualified people are constantly being searched for.

—*Thomas D. Garner*, General Secretary, United Church Press, United Church of Christ.

There are now fewer jobs in denominational offices of communication than there were five, or even three years ago.... In most denominations the communication offices have been the first to receive budget cuts resulting from across the board decreased giving by local churches.

—*Everett G. Parker*, Director, Office of Communication. United Church of Christ.

(See also two related reports in Chapter 10.)

risen above second or third class in quality. It still is true that physically the average church periodical does not bear comparison with the average secular publication often reaching the same readers; until production costs lower, circulations rise, and advertising revenue mounts considerably, the church press may never bear such comparison. No religious body is to be blamed for not producing a periodical as technically excellent as *Horizon* or *House and Garden*. But there is no excuse for questionable advertising, for numerous printing errors, for dull writing, and for playing politics with the denomination's printing press. Church publications should be better written, edited, printed, sold, and read. Here is an exciting opportunity.

All the basic techniques and methods of the secular publications are used by the religious ones. Thus first-class training and sound experience, if sought and adequately rewarded by religious publishing groups, will to an important extent improve the religious communications of the United States and Canada and other parts of the world where they may be needed.

Likewise, the religiously motivated worker in the areas of publicity and public relations, the teaching of religious communications, the religious news and feature syndicates, religious book publishing, missionary or literacy communications, and all the other fields already mentioned can perform great services in the name of the religious communicators' particular faith.

The careers of two young men whose real names are not being used will illustrate further the points in this section. Both attended the same Midwestern school of journalism. Ralph Price gave no thought to religion.

The Job Situation

Perhaps it would be more nearly correct to say that he thought about it, now and then, but brushed it away as only "superstitious nonsense." He had no intention of letting any religion—and he assumed, of course, that he knew what they all stand for—serve as a force in his young life. His goal was to place himself foremost, to gain the most powerful position possible. His aim, as soon as he could achieve it, was to be financially independent, to have the most comfortable and well-equipped home available, and to achieve recognition in the literary world. The latter he hoped to reach by using communications as a stepping-stone.

If, in the course of realizing his ambitions, Ralph had to injure others—that was too bad, he said, but so it had to be. You realize that this world is a competitive one, he used to say. He did not object to unethical conduct, declaring that if he did not take advantage of some other person or situation someone else would do so anyway. Plagiarism, distorting the news, and breaking the copyright laws were among the mildest of his practices. He started as a newspaper reporter, switched to radio news, and settled down as a radio-television junior executive—and to boredom and constant complaint about his job. Decades later his life remains barren, selfish, and purposeless; nor does he have the satisfactions he desired.

On the other hand, there was Channing Stone. He was kindly, considerate, and clearly determined to combine his religious zeal with some sort of communications work. Whereas Ralph was boastful and self-centered, Channing was self-effacing and quiet, almost too pale a personality. But he was no Milquetoast; he spoke up when it was time to defend his views. Ralph spent more hours in scheming to evade his responsibilities than he would consume had he lived up to them. Chan did his work without fuss. He made mistakes, but it was competent work and entirely his own.

Chan Stone wished deeply to serve his denomination, a small one not prepared to pay him much of a salary. He wanted to serve it through journalism. With his dependability, his high work standards, and his gift for writing and editing, he could have had many a good secular job. He had read his denomination's church paper most of his life; he could think of nothing more satisfying than to be connected with it. He had arranged that long before graduation. He is on it today in a position of high responsibility. And he continues to ignore the chances for high salary and great personal glory outside the church. He is what commonly is called a dedicated person; he has a high mission in life.

The calls for help come from what William F. McDermott, who for many years was a full-time free-lance writer, called "an attractive and important field." (See the report in Chapter 10 based on a current survey of denominational and other offices.) Mr. McDermott, the details of whose career are told elsewhere in this book, was for two decades religious news editor of a major daily and contributed to most of the nation's leading popular magazines and many of its religious publications. He wrote these words for this book:

"The world of religion has as much drama, suspense, inspiration, and struggle in it as any other phase of human thought or activity. The field is rich in writing potentialities, and no one with imagination and zeal for finding it will be disappointed if he works hard enough at it."

The Job Situation

Religious journalists believe that writing should be an adventure, never a chore—"not that there isn't hard work or drudgery in it, but one's viewpoint should be illuminated by the fact that it is a great adventure, and one should keep that in mind always."

Mr. McDermott also warns the aspiring writer on religion that "one should expect hard knocks, many rejections, and be prepared to take whatever comes." But one must believe what he is writing, or it won't carry interest or conviction, he insists.

"One should be alive to life, that is, emotionally responsive to the world today as well as to the past."

For further reading about the need for and responsibilities of religious communicators see:

BOOKS AND PAMPHLETS

James Aronson, *Deadline for the Media: Today's Challenges to Press, TV, and Radio.* Indianapolis: Bobbs-Merrill, 1972.

George L. Bird and Frederic E. Merwin, *The Press and Society.* New York: Prentice-Hall, 1951. Revised. Reprinted, 1972, Westport, Conn.: Greenwood.

Church Occupations and Voluntary Service. Nashville: Board of Higher Education and Ministry, The United Methodist Church, 1976. (Pamphlet.)

Robert Cirino, *Don't Blame the People.* Los Angeles: Diversity Press, 1971.

J. Edward Gerald, *Social Responsibilites of the Press.* Minneapolis: University of Minnesota Press, 1963.

A. J. Liebling, *The Press.* New York: Ballantine Books, 1961.

Curtis D. MacDougall, *The Press and Its Problems.* Dubuque, Iowa: Brown, 1964.

A. Kent MacDougall, *The Press*, Princeton, N.J.: Dow Jones Books, 1972.

Martin E. Marty, *The Improper Opinion.* Philadelphia, Pa.: Westminster, 1961.

Martin E. Marty, John G. Deedy, Jr., and David W. Silverman, *The Religious Press in America.* New York: Holt, Rinehart & Winston, 1963.

William L. Rivers and Wilbur Schramm, *Responsibility in Mass Communication.* New York: Harper & Row, 1969. Revised.

Peter M. Sandman, David M. Rubin and David B. Sachsman, eds. *Media Casebook.* Englewood Cliffs, N.J., 1977. Second edition.

Leonard L. Sellers, and William L. Rivers. *Mass Media Issues: Articles and Commentaries.* Englewood Cliffs, N.J.: Prentice-Hall, 1977.

Roland E. Wolseley, *The Changing Magazine.* New York: Hastings House, 1973.

ARTICLES

"Book Ends—Religious Books." *The New York Times Book Review*, May 23, 1976.

Edward B. Fiske, "Religion—Hard Times for the Church Press." *The New York Times*, July 19, 1970.

Alan Geyer, "On the State of Church Journalism." *News Pulse*, April 17, 1970.

Earl C. Gottschalk, Jr., "Career in Journalism Is Now Goal of Many; Job Market Is Glutted." *The Wall Street Journal*, January 19, 1976.

Ernest C. Hynds, "News Coverage of Religions Is Growing." *Editor & Publisher*, October 18, 1975.

4 On the Secular Job

Soon after Arlene Miller had settled down at her desk to open the envelopes to "Church Editor," "Religious Reporter," or just "Church Department," the one-eyed blinker near her typewriter became excited.

Pastor Jones was on the telephone again. He had called her at home, at breakfast, already. Alvin Arthur Jones was one of the most persistent of her news sources. In her less charitable moments she also thought of him as something of a pest.

"Miss Miller," he said this time, "I'm sorry to bother you again, but I forgot one thing. Please include Mrs. Arthur's name in the committee lists I gave you this morning, won't you?"

"Yes, of course," she said, and then quickly asked, "Which Mrs. Arthur, Mr. Jones? Mrs. James or Mrs.

John? And which committee, the bazaar or the dinner? There's a Mrs. Arthur on each, you know."

Mr. Jones quickly explained that it was Mrs. James and that she was on the bazaar committee. Arlene dutifully noted that and, as soon as the conversation was over, made the copy conform. Then she returned to her envelope-slitting. But the blue plastic had hardly torn through the flap of the first one she picked up when a shadow deepened over her desk and a visitor stood before her.

Arlene knew this visitor well; this smiling lady with the lavender-tinged white hair came at least weekly to leave news stories about the Council of Church Women. They were usable stories, too, carefully written and typed, with the lead facts usually where they belonged. Arlene rarely had to do more than verify a name spelling. The copy's excellent condition was not surprising, for the smartly dressed woman now beside her once had been assistant city editor of a large daily. Ever since her marriage and her retirement from newspaper work, Mrs. Palmer had kept her professional skill alive by serving as head of the publicity committee for one group or another: first the church women's organization, then the whole congregation, and now the religiously active women of the entire city.

Unlike many of Arlene's visitors, Mrs. Palmer never stayed too long. She was businesslike. Arlene suspected that she brought the copy instead of mailing it only because she enjoyed so much reentering the newspaper city room. But she did not overwork her sentimental feeling and become a nuisance. After a few brisk, friendly words she left Arlene to her duties.

On the Secular Job

All in the Day's Work

As the afternoon passed, Arlene (an improvised name for a religion editor friend of the author who had these experiences) had more telephone calls and visitors, not all from church people by any means. For she also covered clubs for the morning daily on which she worked. Part of the time she clung to the phone herself, dialing a series of numbers in search of news. Some calls were to church secretaries, others to volunteer publicity chairmen, and still others to officers of interfaith groups. She was collecting news for immediate use and also to help her produce an attractive Saturday religion page.

In that mail she was opening she found the daily report from Religious News Service, a main source of facts about religious happenings outside her own city. Also there were various publicity stories from the World Council of Churches, the National Council of Churches, various small and large denominational public relations offices—Catholic, Jewish, Protestant—that wished to keep her informed of their activities. Occasionally she saw a chance for a local feature.

One was the story she had used some weeks back about the refugee family taken in by a couple that had made room in an attic for the almost penniless mother, father, and three young daughters.

And so her day went—extending into the evening. She mixed news gathering by phone with personal stops at regular news source offices, going sometimes by bus and other times in her own small car. She once estimated that she had eaten five miles of meat loaf and at least one hundred and forty apple pies—whole pies, not just slices—in her five years on this job. She had to spend many hours at church suppers. She gulped the typical tasty home-cooked but fattening church dinner food while a photographer snapped the speaker and several officers, a sale progressing at a booth, the women of the general committee looking at lists on a table, or the new officers smiling at the camera.

Although her copy was double-checked by the news editor, Arlene did all her own writing and editing, including headlines and makeup. She kept her own appointment book; requested the photographer's services as she thought wise; cropped, sized, and captioned pictures herself; assembled and edited the publicity and syndicated material; and did other routine jobs of a religious news editor who also must cover the city's clubs.

A Typical Situation

Arlene Miller's activities are typical of those on any small secular daily that publishes church and religious news. (The difference? *Church* news is about organized religions; *religious* news is about the philosophy known as religion.) Only a few large, metropolitan papers give religious editors one or two assistants who report stories, handle certain desk duties, and take care of makeup and record keeping. The schedule is different for an afternoon paper than for a morning one, for a weekly than for a daily. The religion news editor of a news service has similar routines, but he or she is concerned about religion news on a national and international scale instead of on a local or community level. The persons responsible for this kind of news for syndicates, broadcasting stations, and magazines are few, but these too must report, select, write, sort, assemble, and present the news in the way their media require. Arlene Miller writes for the eye; the pastor or layman who prepares a weekly religious news broadcast writes for the ear. The techniques of news gathering are the same, but those of news presentation differ by medium.

If Arlene Miller were on one of the largest papers, she would sit, not before a typewriter, but in front of a video terminal, which is a silent electric typewriter keyboard with a television screen at the top instead of paper. What the reporter writes appears on the screen. The terminal is connected to a central computer that records the words typed by the reporter.

The more than seven hundred men and women who serve as church and religion news writers and editors for American dailies, the newsmagazines, and the news agencies are the core of the corps of religious communicators who work on the staffs of secular publications. A small percentage of them began the work without previous communications experience. Most came from other media-related jobs, usually as reporters—police, club, education, or some other beat common in communications.

A Pioneer and His Followers

The careers of individuals may be revealing and encouraging. The life stories of the early religious journalists and those of today contrast deeply. One pioneer was William Bernard Norton, for a quarter of a century religion editor of the Chicago *Tribune*. He won a permanent place for himself with his work and his book, *Church and Newspaper*.

Dr. Norton was better educated, at least formally, than

most of today's writers and editors in his specialty. Born in Illinois in 1857, he earned his bachelor's, master's, and doctor's degrees before becoming an Iowa and Illinois pastor. In the two final years of his pastoral career he wrote for the Chicago City News Bureau and then became editor of *The Methodist Episcopal Advocate*, a monthly magazine later renamed *The Christian Advocate*. He held that position from 1910 to 1919. Simultaneously he was religion editor of the *Tribune*. His devotion to religious journalism led him to establish in 1936 a lectureship in church and newspapers at Garrett-Evangelical Theological Seminary (then Garrett Biblical Institute), his own institution. He died the same year.

The list of outstanding church and religion editors of the times is long, too long to be complete here. Careers of such editors, past and present, are worth study. This can be done through such reference books as *Who's Who in America*, similar regional volumes, *Who's Who of American Women*, and *Working Press of the Nation*. Here are a few names as a starter, with the titles of the publications or agencies with which they have been most closely related; some no longer are living:

Lillian Block, managing editor and senior vice-president, Religious News Service
James W. Carty, Jr., Nashville *Tennessean*
Louis Cassels, United Press International
John Cogley, *The New York Times*
George W. Cornell, Associated Press
William Dinwoodie, Cleveland *News*
George Dugan, *The New York Times*
Terry Ferrer, *Newsweek*
William Folger, Buffalo *Evening News*
Harrison Fry, Philadelphia *Bulletin*

Helen Gott Gray, Kansas City *Star*
Marjorie Hyer, Washington *Post*
Lester Kinsolving, syndicated columnist
Caspar Nannes, Washington *Star*
Richard Ostling, *Time*
Richard B. Philbrick, Chicago *Tribune*
Ann Elizabeth Price, New York *Herald Tribune*
William A. Reed, Jr., Nashville *Tennessean*
Ruth E. Riley, Kansas City (Kan.) *Kansan*
Ora Spaid, Louisville *Courier Journal*
Frank Stewart, Cleveland *Press*
John T. Stewart, St. Louis *Post-Dispatch*
Adon Taft, Miami *Herald*
Willmar L. Thorkelson, Minneapolis *Star*
Dan L. Thrapp, Los Angeles *Times*
Margaret A. Vance, Newark *News*
Richard Wager, Cleveland *Plain Dealer*
Hiley Ward, Detroit *Free-Press*
Robert Whitaker, Providence *Journal*
Lance Zavits, Buffalo *Evening News*

The careers of several of these men and women are worth more detail here, beginning with one, a minister's son who has been in religious journalism during his entire career. He is George Dugan, who began as a reporter for the *Presbyterian Tribune*. He next served on the Protestant desk of Religious News Service for eight years; from there he went to *The New York Times,* serving as religious news editor from 1949 to 1965 and religious news reporter since. His *Times* work has brought him the Religious Public Relations Council's Award of Merit. He also has won the James O. Supple Memorial Award given by the Religion Newswriters Association annually for the best work in the field. He has covered virtually all important religious meetings for several decades all over the world.

BIOGRAPHICAL BACKGROUND
Special Assignment Reporter

Some of the journalists who cover religion are religious, others make no pretensions of having religious beliefs, and still others think whether they are personally followers of a particular religion is irrelevant. A science writer is not necessarily scientific, the latter point out, adding that such writers rarely are scientists, although they are expected to understand the world of science. An education reporter presumably is educated but need not carry a label of being a follower of one or the other philosophy of religion.

But there are sincere religious persons on communications staffs who write or edit outside the field of religion yet try to put their views into practice by their conduct and their personal attitudes toward the assignments. They work in the secular world but have their own motives.

One such is McCandlish Phillips, from 1950 to 1975 a member of the New York *Times* staff, much of that time a special assignment reporter. He was hired by the *Times* at first as a copyboy, although he had worked for several small newspapers earlier, in Boston's suburbs. He then was 24. Ten years later he had become one of the *Times'* highest ranking reporters.

Journalism, in a way, was what attracted Phillips to the church. While he was working in Boston another newsman, a friend, asked him to go to church with him one day. He has been an active churchman ever since.

Phillips has covered both religious and secular stories over the intervening years; often they have been the kind involving human interest, such as the account of the rescue of the crew of a sunken tanker. Another was the story of Daniel Burros, a Nazi and some years ago head of the New York activities of the Ku Klux Klan. That article gained him three journalism awards, for it was a dangerous assignment.

Phillips tried to help Burros by quoting 2 Corinthians 5:17 to him, which reads: "If any man be in Christ, he is a new creature: old things are passed away; behold, all things are become new."

Burros refused to listen. Later, he committed suicide.

One of McCandlish Phillips' books, *City Notebook*, records some of his experiences as a newsman. Its focus is life in New York City, where he has worked for so many years. In 1970 he published another book, *The Bible, the Supernatural, and the Jews*. Since 1975 he has written only occasionally for the *Times*.

Both his life and his journalism are worth study. They show how the religious writer must be a first-class craftsman in addition to everything else.

One of the founders of the Religion Newswriters Association (hereafter called RNA) was Caspar Nannes. By the time he became its president in 1956 he had gone on to win various awards for his work on the Washington *Star*. Nannes is one of the few PhD degree holders to serve as a religion editor. He was a member of the Rutgers University English department faculty for eight years and of the same department at the University of Illinois for three. A Rutgers Phi Beta Kappa, he received his master's from there and his doctorate from the University of Pennsylvania.

Nannes began his journalistic career with the *Star* in 1943, becoming religion news editor in 1949. In 1965 he was named winner of the first annual R. S. Reynolds Award, given by the Presbyterian Church in the United States for "excellence in religious news coverage." Before this he had received the Religious Public Relations Council (RPRC) Award of Merit as well as the Award in Religious Communication from the Religious Heritage of America.

The religious news editor of another nationally important daily, the Minneapolis *Star*, is Willmar L. Thorkelson. He was still a boy when Dr. Norton had been the Chicago *Tribune*'s church editor. He entered religious journalism via journalistic, not religious, work. At Concordia College in Minnesota he edited the college weekly; he received a BA cum laude in 1940.

Bill Thorkelson's first job was as city hall and courthouse reporter, sports editor, and feature writer for the *Tribune* in Bismarck, North Dakota. After nine months on that daily he moved to Detroit Lakes to become assistant editor of another *Tribune*, published in that town. Nine months later he left to enroll at the School of Journalism of the University of Minnesota, serving as an assistant while earning his master's degree.

That fall he joined the Minneapolis *Star* and *Tribune*, working for these sister papers as a general assignment reporter. Since 1944 he has been their religion news expert except for occasional stints as city hall and legislature writer. By 1954 he was editing the *Star*'s religious news pages and writing a column, "This Week in Religion." He has covered the major meetings of religious bodies in various parts of the globe. He, too, has been awarded honors for his religious news coverage, receiving the RPRC and Supple awards.

Even during a year's leave of absence in the late 1940s he was engaged in religious communications work: as press officer for the World Council of Churches, in its Geneva, Switzerland, headquarters. For the past three decades he has written, as well, for *Christian Herald* and other magazines and served as *The Christian Century*'s Minnesota correspondent.

EDITOR/PUBLISHER

An Editor/Publisher Gives Space to Religion

"Jesus Christ is a teacher at Camp Koinonia"

" 'Word of God' Echoes at Bundy's Bridge"

Such headlines are not commonly found in a secular newspaper. Those and others like them appear almost weekly in the Sweet Home (Ore.) *The New Era,* a standard, 8-column paper which covers all the other usual stories of a small town as well: the courts, the street department, education developments, weddings, and deaths, among many other events.

This unusual small paper published in the state's Linn County was established almost fifty years ago. But since Dave Cooper, its editor and publisher, bought it in 1974, religious news has been getting unusual play. And Cooper learned that the townspeople appreciate it, even though the area is not known

Other Prominent Writers

Another major figure in religious news work was Rachel McDowell, who for about thirty years served *The New York Times* as religion news editor, giving it eminence in that field equal to its high reputation for excellent coverage in other subjects. Miss McDowell confined herself to print journalism.

Ann Elizabeth Price, later Mrs. Harry Baehr, while long in experience as a writer about religion, continues to work as a free-lance in the field. She can trace her abilities in part to the fact that she is of a journalistic family. Canadian born, she was the daughter of staffers on the Calgary *Albertan;* her mother was society editor

as particularly religion-conscious.

Religion, Cooper says, changed his life. It was no instant conversion. He admits that he had been a heavy drinker and smoker and had alienated his family before he was converted. He bought the paper and through it attempts to call attention to the power of Christianity in the individual's life while at the same time doing a competent job of covering the rest of the news and presenting it attractively.

The editor and publisher usually writes these religious stories himself, signs them, and takes the pictures to accompany them.

The one headlined, "Jesus Christ is a teacher at Camp Koinonia," ran on the first page, covering a third of the sheet, and filled all of the fourth page. It is the story of a Christian church camp in Oregon. Another headed, "The Story of an Unfulfilled Dream," is about a local country preacher, a young man, who wants to be a missionary. It is not an unsuccess story but reveals the pro-

---

and her father sports editor. Her name is Jo-Ann; one paper objected, saying it sounded like a cooking writer's.

She started her journalistic life at fifteen, as a high school correspondent for the Vancouver *Daily Province*. While studying at the University of British Columbia she wrote for that paper and joined its staff in the summer. She left Canada to enter the Medill School of Journalism at Northwestern University as a sophomore. She received her bachelor's degree with distinction and won a scholarship that financed her master's in journalism.

Her first American job was as a reporter-photographer for the Amarillo, Texas, *Times*. Within two months she turned north again to become a general reporter for the Milwaukee *Journal*. Until then, she has said, it never occurred to her to become a religious writer.

blems of persons with such hopes. It includes four pictures and occupies more than a fourth of page one and a half of page four.

Christmas, of course, is a big day for *The New Era*. On that day it resembles the more conventional country paper in its treatment of the religious event, for most such community publications say little about religion except on special occasions of this type. A local pastor contributed to the *Era*'s editorial page a piece entitled "The Irony, Tragedy, and Blessedness of Christmas."

Dave Cooper's own column, "Cooper's Jug," tells the story of his changed life. Looking back over the fateful preceding year he writes: "But it is His will that I be with Christ this Christmas and that thought brings me joy. Nothing could make this Christmas more special than to be in the company of the King." A Christmas picture and a Christmas cartoon decorate the page beside the usual letters to the editor, a municipal court report, and several news stories.

"I had no particular interest in the field of religious journalism," she later admitted, "since I had a general news background and, if anything, did not want to specialize."

But specialize she did, for in 1946 she was asked to be religion news editor "because the man who did that work was leaving the paper," she explains. Her paper sent her to Europe in 1950 to cover religion in six countries and to take pictures. She has been at it ever since.

The shift to New York City came the next year. In 1951 she occupied one of the top positions in religious news work in America—religious news editor for the prestigious New York *Herald Tribune*. Within a year she had won a George Polk Memorial Award for "Outstanding Religious News Reporting." Other major awards followed: the Supple, the Religious Heritage, the RPRC.

Mrs. Baehr left the *Herald Tribune* in 1965 to free lance. She now is the wife of a retired *Herald Tribune* editorial writer, Harry Baehr, who also is an author. Mrs. Baehr's articles appear occasionally in *The New York Times* and other publications. In 1975 she covered the World Council of Churches Assembly in Nairobi, Kenya, for the National Catholic News Service and other clients.

Louis Cassels, served for 32 years with United Press International, one of the two major news agencies of the world. He was its religion news editor from 1956 to his death in 1974.

He was one of the most distinguished of the journalists in his specialty. His influence was wider than that of most religion writers. His material went simultaneously to hundreds of publications and other media.

The respect and affection felt for him by his colleagues were reflected in the messages received by the Religion Newswriters Association at his death. Magazines and newspapers of religion published tributes and church leaders from many denominations expressed their admiration. His ashes were immured in a niche of Bethlehem Chapel in Washington Cathedral, a rare honor accorded earlier to President Woodrow Wilson, John R. Mott, Helen Keller, and other notables.

Minorities Come to the Fore

Minorities, particularly women and members of the black race, are finding more places on secular publication staffs year by year, governed to some extent by the state of the economy. They are not many, as yet, but at least are on the increase.

On the Secular Job

On daily newspapers that employ church and religious news writers and editors, for example, women for many years have held such positions, perhaps because women often are more active in church work than men. That situation continues today.

But we now see a few of these jobs going as well to black men and women, a much less common occurrence. Among them, in the general press, are William A. Reed, Jr., 1976-77 president of the Religion Newswriters Association and religion news editor of the Nashville *Tennessean* (see Biographical Background elsewhere in this chapter); Mrs. Helen Gott Gray, a graduate of the School of Public Communications at Syracuse University; she was Helen Theresa Gott in the early 1960s when she studied in Syracuse and planned to go in for a magazine journalism career; she soon went to the Kansas City *Star* as a reporter, and then got the religion beat; and Lynn Norman, who covers religion for the Memphis *Commercial Appeal*.

Black-owned newspapers occasionally can afford to hire religion writers and editors; several of these papers, most of which are weeklies, have won distinction through the work of their religion staffers. Among them are Birdie M. Jackson, of the East St. Louis (Ill.) *Crusader;* Robbie L. McCoy, Detroit *Michigan Chronicle;* and Virgie W. Murray, Los Angeles *Sentinel*. All three belong to the RNA.

At least eight more of the newspapers published for Afro-Americans have their own religion editors, according to a check made for this book by Sherman Briscoe, executive director emeritus of the National Newspaper Publishers Association. Since the approximately two hundred black papers are mainly small weeklies, the positions naturally are on the larger publications. The editors and papers recorded by Mr. Briscoe are:

Pam Widgeon, Baltimore *Afro-American;* Irene Beckwith, Washington *Afro-American;* Dorothy A. Draib, Chicago *Daily Defender;* Leona Tompkins, San Francisco *Sun-Reporter;* Barbara Drury, St. Louis *Argus;* Loretta Cowan, Cleveland *Call & Post;* Willa Mae Rice, New Pittsburgh *Courier;* and Willa Thomas, Indianapolis *Recorder.*

This press, which is owned, operated, produced, and intended solely for black persons, also includes a few religious magazines as well as about fifteen secular radio stations and around two hundred secular magazines. Most black media tend to give religion considerable time and space.

Radio and Television

Full-time posts as religious radio or television writer or editor are rare for single stations or networks. Here and there church officials or lay persons go into such stations at set hours to broadcast religious news or arrange telecasts, usually as volunteers. Religion still commands much more attention from the printed media than from the electronic. The reasons for this are economic, philosophical, and technical. Printing is cheaper than broadcasting; whereas publications are receiving more and more revenue from sales of copies and becoming less dependent therefore upon advertising, electronic communications receives no such direct support from the listener or viewer (except as gifts to public stations). Traditionally broadcasting, being a mass medium, is

On location during a Protestant Radio and Television Center filming of a documentary in Mexico; both Mexican and American film crews are at work.

restrained as printed journalism is not. A publication can be kept out of sight but a radio or television set is harder to control. Furthermore, broadcasting is licensed and printed communications is not.

Through a few dozen stations of their own, religious groups make constantly more use of the airwaves. More attention is given, however, to preparing materials for use by nonreligious stations or in overseas programs. Nevertheless, persons capable of doing the work involved in any aspect of electronic communications are appreciated in the religious communications world, comparatively few as the positions may be at any one time. Thus would-be workers in this area are wise to learn how to write news copy, plan television and radio programs about religious news events, gain experience in camera

BIOGRAPHICAL BACKGROUND

From College Paper Editor to Head of Religion Writers

When William A. Reed, Jr., religious news editor of the Nashville *Tennessean,* was a student at Fisk University, he served as editor of the Fisk *Herald.* One of his predecessors in the job was Dr. W. E. B. Du Bois, the noted sociologist and journalist who founded five magazines in his day, two of which still are published.

Since college, Bill Reed has had a diversified career, but mainly within the communications field. He has worked in public relations, as a news writer and editor, and in circulation and advertising. He also was a railway mail clerk much of the time and now is retired from that U.S. government job.

His editorial work has been for four newspapers, all widely known: as reporter for the Atlanta *Daily World,* the first Black daily to survive; as a correspondent for the Norfolk *Journal & Guide;* as state correspondent for the Afro-American Newspapers, a large chain of black weeklies and semiweeklies on the East Coast; and from 1961 to 1965 as reporter for the *Tennessean,* and since 1965 its religious news editor.

Earlier he had been circulation manager and columnist for the Nashville *Defender,* display advertising salesman for the Nashville *Globe,* and advertising manager for another Nashville paper, the *News-Star.* His marketing work was done for coffee and bakery firms, the public relations for the Nashville Housing Authority, the Board of Evangelism of the United Methodist Church, and as news editor of *The Upper Room,* the multimillion circulation devotional magazine of that denomination.

In 1976-77 he served as president of the Religion Newswriters Association. During his career he has been honored with citations from

> Baptist, Seventh-day Adventist, regional and community groups, and made a Fellow of the Religious Public Relations Council.
>
> An American Baptist, he has been active in the senior citizens work of Nashville, serving as a board member from 1969 to 1972.
>
> Writing about Bill Reed's work at the *Tennessean* in the RNA *News Letter*, L. F. Heins, the *News Letter*'s editor, said:
>
> "A few years ago he broke a story which received national attention—the recall of a Baptist youth publication for printing a photograph of an interracial couple. More recently Bill researched in Massachusetts and Pennsylvania to trace the beginnings of evangelistic work by one Jimmy Carter, Southern Baptist, now residing in Plains, Ga."

techniques and in the preparation and uses of cassettes and tapes. Since most religious programming has to do with sermons, discussions, drama, worship services, panels, and other noncommunications programs, knowledge of that kind of programming is valuable.

A few religious news scripts, mostly assemblies of news and feature stories, are provided by syndicates or public relations offices of religious bodies. Occasionally a local station gives church groups time to disseminate religious news. Here, too, are opportunities, on a paid or volunteer basis, for these organizations need knowledgeable personnel from time to time.

Secular-owned and operated stations would provide more than the small amount of public service time now devoted to religion if they had greater assurance of listening and if competent persons more often would offer to provide talent. Such stations also need to be convinced that all religious broadcasting need not be concentrated in Sunday time bands and seasonal periods like religious holidays. Another barrier may be lack of sponsorship.

Religious communicators, whatever their medium, can move up in the ranks of the secular run media to other positions. One reporter eventually became city editor and then chief editorial writer of a large Midwestern daily. Another was made assistant city editor of his paper after five years on the religion beat. A third, always holding to his religious principles, became publisher of a large daily and won a Pulitzer Prize for his investigative reporting and editorial position. Numbers of others have been appointed top editors in church publishing houses or placed in vital administrative posts in foreign fields, having moved into these positions from the secular world of communications.

The Pulitzer Prize winner mentioned above is Harold E. Martin, editor and publisher of the Montgomery (Ala.) *Advertiser—Alabama Journal.* Martin obtained a master's degree from a school of journalism which emphasized graphic arts and religious journalism. He had come to his studies with considerable practical experience in production work. Even while studying he worked in newspaper composing rooms. After working for newspapers on the production side he joined the dailies in Montgomery.

It was there that, in 1970, he won the Pulitzer Award, in special local reporting. Always a strong church worker, he also has become known as a fighting editor, concerned to expose corruption, support social justice, and assist in community development.

In 1976 he won the Alabama Baptist Communications Award for his "contribution to Christianity through religious journalism." The next year he was elected president of Multimedia Newspapers; he became responsible for newspapers in Greenville, S.C., Asheville, N.C., Clarksville, N.C., and seventeen non-dailies elsewhere.

For further reading about being on the secular job:

BOOKS

Richard Terrill Baker, *The Christian as a Journalist.* New York: Association Press, 1961.

Mitchell V. Charnley, *Reporting.* New York: Holt, Rinehart & Winston, 1975. Third edition.

John L. Fell, *Film: An Introduction.* New York: Praeger, 1975.

Robert L. Hilliard, ed., *Understanding Television.* New York: Hastings House, 1974.

Curtis D. MacDougall, *Interpretative Reporting.* New York: Macmillan, 1977. Seventh edition.

William Bernard Norton, *Church and Newspaper.* New York: Macmillan, 1930.

Roland E. Wolseley, *Understanding Magazines.* Ames: Iowa State University Press, 1969. Second edition.

ARTICLES

Rick Friedman, "On the Job: The Religion Writer." *Editor & Publisher,* October 14, 1961.

George Gent, "Priest Doffs His Clerical Garb to Seek Career as TV Newsman." *The New York Times,* April 19, 1969.

Helen E. Hull, "Editors Hear *Times* Reporter at

Wheaton." *Just Between Us*, January 1968. (About McCandlish Phillips.)

Charles C. Hushaw, "Religion Is Their News Beat." *The Lutheran*, January 30, 1963.

Religion Newswriters Association *News Letter*. Various issues of this monthly contain reports on working methods and conditions of RNS members.

"Reporter on a Story." *Power Life for Older Teens*, February 19, 1967. (About McCandlish Phillips.)

RNA, a brief history of the Religion Newswriters Association. 1974. (Pamphlet.)

Ruth E. Riley, "I Was a Church News Editor." *Modern Maturity*, December-January, 1972-73.

5 On the Religious Job

Influenced by the story of the Watergate exposé written by two investigative reporters, Carl Bernstein and Robert Woodward of the Washington *Post*, would-be journalists have flocked to the schools of journalism and communications since the early 1970s. The books by these two hardworking reporters and the motion picture based on one of their other books have moved men and women alike to become investigative reporters for any of the media receptive to them.

But few Watergate stories break in a nation's history. Communications work more often is routine, even boring at times, rather than exciting. If it were so constantly arousing as portrayed in most books and screen shows about journalism, little work would be done. In all communications, routines must govern because accurate and readable new stories, features, articles, fiction, and departmental copy cannot be produced dependably otherwise. Nor can pictures and cartoons appear without regular and steady work. The now more and more electronic composing rooms must work on schedules as well. Only systematic planning will achieve production of a publication or provision of reading or illustrated matter in time for editors or broadcasters to use it.

The workday in a religious publication or news agency office is so much like that in a secular one that a casual visitor would hardly know the difference. If one walks into the Religious News Service offices at 43 W. 57th Street in New York City only three clues reveal the fact that it is a newsgathering and disseminating organization dealing exclusively with news of the religious world. Catholic, Jewish, and Protestant publications are about. In the reference book collection are many about religion, far more than in the usual newsroom morgue. And if one glances at any of the copy being produced one notes that all the stories have to do with religion in some way. Other religious news and feature services, such as the National Catholic News Service, function along standard lines insofar as they can with limited staff and small budgets.

Similarly, if one stops at the offices of *The Lutheran*, *Christian Century*, or *The Sign*, for example, they are not markedly different from those of other small specialized magazines. They are dramatically less plush and well-to-do than those of *Time*, *Ebony*, or *Reader's Digest*, to be sure, but they, too, depend upon file cases, typewriters, reference books, news that arrives by mail and machine; they too receive articles, news stories, and photographs from free-lancers and agencies and publicity offices.

Similar Titles

The writers and editors who have to do with the journalistic expression of religion hold more or less the same titles and do about the same kinds of work as do secular communicators. The subjects and motivation differ, the taboos may be more numerous for the person in religious work, the editorial policies are not necessarily the same, but there is little in the appearance and the performance of duties that marks off the religious journalist or communicator. Certain special personal and vocational problems do exist, however.

The few religious journalists who have written about their work have said little concerning what life is like in their surroundings. They were far more concerned about their objectives and ideals. This inattention to their everyday activities suggests that those activities never were extraordinary enough to be worth mentioning. It also may explain why, during its history, the bulk of religious journalism in this country has been below par technically. Religious communicators either have known or cared so little about communications as communications that they scarcely have considered themselves communicators. More often than not they have been like editors of so many American country newspapers, who usually think of themselves as printers or businessmen, not journalists and certainly not communicators.

Yet the outstanding publications invariably have been in the hands of persons concerned about technically high-quality journalism. Ford Stewart and Kenneth Wilson, and before them Daniel Poling and Clarence Hall, of the Christian Herald Association have thought it important to make their magazine arresting in appearance and compelling in writing style. G. Elson Ruff, while editor of *The Lutheran,* constantly sought to improve that magazine, as his successor, Alfred P. Stauderman, has since his own appointment. Kyle Haselden, Dean Peerman, and Margaret Frakes, and before them Charles Clayton Morrison, Paul Hutchinson, and Harold Fey of the *Christian Century,* as limited in budget as are most publication executives in the religious world, for many years provided readers with the best of religious world news coverage obtainable in such periodicals. The most recent editors of this weekly, Alan Geyer, Martin E. Marty (although the latter has served the magazine since the mid-1950s), and James M. Wall have followed in the tradition.

Erwin Canham and the other former editors of the *Christian Science Monitor,* one of the world's outstanding general newspapers but published by a church body from the days of Willis J. Abbot to the present, did meticulous editorial work. Edward S. Skillen, successor to the influential Michael Williams, and his staff made *Commonweal* an effective voice of a segment of the Roman Catholic laity in the Williams tradition; it is continued to this day.

Merely to look at others, typified by *A.D., The Critic, Commentary, The Sign, The Churchman, Home Life,* and *Home Missions,* shows that behind these periodicals stand persons with respect for ability with journalistic skills.

As individuals, these and other widely recognized religious journalists have been professional writers and editors. Occasionally a churchman, taken from the pulpit or the seminary faculty, heads a publication without benefit of journalistic experience or training and achieves the influence gained by those carefully prepared for journalistic responsibilities. Usually the inside story is that this editor has leaned for years upon the knowledge of colleagues, who have been the real editors all along.

The Paths to Prominence

Before they reached prominence, what were the paths of some of those persons mentioned thus far?

G. Elson Ruff had secular journalistic experience before going to the staff of his church's publication. He was a reporter on the Philadelphia *Inquirer* and other newspapers, becoming editor of *The Lutheran* in 1945. The next year he also assumed the editorship of Fortress Press (then called Muhlenberg Press), the book publishing arm of his denomination. When the magazine became a large biweekly through the merger of several Lutheran denominations, Dr. Ruff left the book work.

Another who followed the method of Elson Ruff was Dr. Guy Emery Shipler, editor of *The Churchman* for many years. This vigorous, independent Episcopal magazine now edited by his longtime assistant, Edna Ruth Johnson, is one of the oldest periodicals of any kind in the United States. Dr. Shipler's first journalism was learned as a reporter on a Rochester, New York, daily, followed by other newspaper work, including that of reporter on the Boston *Traveler*.

Still others who followed the secular journalist path are Robert A. Elfers, Clarence Hall, Robert J. Cadigan, and Lillian R. Block.

Bob Elfers worked on secular newspapers after his graduation from journalism school. For a time he was editor of *Young People* and other American Baptist Churches publications; later he became an editor at Friendship Press, the book publishing arm of the National Council of Churches. From there he went to Association Press, the YMCA's book publishing company, to become assistant director. His present post is that of publications officer of the Girl Scouts at the national offices in New York.

Clarence Hall, at one time a senior editor at *Reader's Digest* and prior to that executive editor of *Christian Herald* and editorial director of *Lifetime Living*, began as a reporter and feature writer for Florida newspapers.

Robert Cadigan had a different vocational start from the others: he was for ten years chairman of a Society of Friends school English department, and then, for two years, associate editor of *Holiday* magazine. He entered religious journalism at *Presbyterian Life*, serving as general manager until 1947 and editor until 1954; his magazine became one of the few of religion that exceeded one million circulation. It did so until economic conditions affected most mainline denominations.

Miss Block, managing editor of Religious News Service since 1957, also went into the career of religious communications from teaching; (she was teaching journalism).

Miss Block made the switch while she was on the faculty of New York University's Department of Journalism. This is how she describes it:

> It was in 1943—in the midst of World War II. My classes at NYU were made up mostly of men. The classes began to grow smaller and smaller as some students enlisted and others were drafted. I was acutely aware that students were more concerned about whether or not they would be alive

six months hence than they were in learning about the history of American journalism, how to write a good news story, feature, or editorial, or how you do a critical review of a book or a play.

I decided to take a leave of absence for the duration and do something more relevant until the war ended. I was on my way to take a job with the public relations department of the Army Air Force when I learned about RNS, then about ten years old. I decided to have a look-see and my conviction grew that real peace in the world would be achieved only by greater understanding of one another. What RNS was doing was unique—and still is—as the only interreligious news agency anywhere. By objective reporting of news of all religious groups, RNS was creating new understanding in the best interest of the public order.

When Louis Minsky, another widely respected religious journalist who was managing editor of RNS during Miss Block's early years with the service, died in 1947 she succeeded him. The service, which is sustained by the National Council of Christians and Jews, was then as it is today, one of the Council's nonprofit activities.

Before teaching at NYU Miss Block had been a reporter for New York and New Jersey newspapers, a writer for professional journals, and editor of a book review syndicate. She was a journalism major at NYU and also had an MA from Columbia University.

Now senior vice-president of the NCCJ, she supervises a large operation for RNS which sells services to about eight hundred clients, supplying both written and photocopy. Her mounting responsibilities brought her the St. Francis de Sales Award of the Catholic Press Association in 1976; St. Francis is considered the patron saint of journalists.

BIOGRAPHICAL BACKGROUND

Magazine Associate Editor Does Free-Lance Writing

Sometimes persons chosen for communications positions in the religious world lack professional qualifications. Those having such qualifications do not always produce work of high quality and those without those qualifications are by no means sure to be failures. But it is more likely, other skills and characteristics being equal, that the person experienced and trained in communications will do better than the neophyte who must learn on the job, and perhaps learn only one way.

Lois Y. Barrett, still in her twenties, was associate editor of *The Mennonite* when this was written. (She has since taken another assignment.) She brought secular journalistic experience to her position in 1971 and had been active in church life from her early years. She also had had some university journalism training. Miss Barrett not only is busy in journalism as an editor and free-lance writer but also is active in civic affairs.

A native of Enid, Oklahoma, she went to elementary schools in Kansas and Texas. Her first journalism courses were taken while she was a high school student at Sweetwater, Texas. From there she went to the University of Oklahoma at Norman. On the university paper, the *Oklahoma Daily*, she held several positions, including those of staff writer, senior reporter, news editor, and managing editor. She received her BA, majoring in psychology but also including

RNS clients include newspapers, news magazines, church publications, radio and television stations, and denominational organs and agencies. It has nine hundred news and photo correspondents in the United States and abroad; these correspondents are almost all part-timers.

eight hours of journalism, in 1969. Theological study followed, first at Brite Divinity School, Texas Christian University, and then at Mennonite Biblical Seminary, for short periods at each.

Professional journalism began for Miss Barrett in the summer of 1968 when she was an intern as a copy editor on the Corpus Christi (Tex.) *Caller-Times*. That was followed by work as a reporter for the Wichita (Kan.) *Eagle*, where she covered the poverty beat, general assignments, and church news.

Originally a member of the Christian Church (Disciples of Christ), she joined a Mennonite congregation in Wichita in 1971 when she went to *The Mennonite's* staff.

This magazine is unusual in that it serves two countries, the United States and Canada. Its editor is in Winnipeg but it is published in Newton, Kansas. It is the weekly of the General Conference Mennonite Church and has 16,000 circulation in the two nations.

On *The Mennonite* Lois Barrett spent half her time, logically enough in view of her training and experience, handling the news section, which meant writing and editing and, as she described it, "overseeing of copyreading, proofreading, and layout of the magazine of the whole." She also wrote some editorials.

The other half of her time she used to edit the General Conference News Service, which also took advantage of her news background. She served as a reporter, writer, and editor of this weekly service for her denomination. It required her to travel in both the States and Canada.

Her free-lancing has led to by-lines in *Christian Living*, *Faith at Work*, *The Wichita Eagle*, *Sojourners*, and *The Other Side*. She wrote a

---

Up to seventy news stories a day are sent out of the New York offices.

Miss Block's conviction about the social value of RNS has not flagged since she joined its staff. "What had happened in the years since," she says, "has increasingly un-

chapter for a study guide on *Women in the Bible and Early Anabaptism,* published in 1975 by the Faith and Life Press. Her section was on "Women in the Anabaptist Movement."

Some of Miss Barrett's civic activities are unusual. She has been a member of the Fairview Mennonite House, an intentional community in Wichita, since 1971. In 1976, she explains, it consisted of eight adults and nine children who share income and property, have a common religious life, and live in one household.

The young editor also belongs to a neighborhood council of the Citizens Participation Organization in Wichita and is corresponding secretary of the Midtown Citizens Association of that city. She directed the youth choir of her church, Lorraine Avenue Mennonite, from 1971 to 1974.

---

dergirded this conviction. I am more involved than ever in the job that I thought would be a temporary one—for the duration of the war."

She considers religious journalism an important field for young people. Speaking at the ceremonies marking the fiftieth anniversary of the School of Journalism at the University of Missouri, she said:

> I know what many of you are thinking right now. You're pretty sure that religious journalism is dull, abstruse—yes, let's admit, even boring. You're convinced that it offers few opportunities, that it is more or less an esoteric branch of the fourth estate, and that it holds out little excitement, adventure, and challenge to your abilities and training. And I'm here to tell you that you couldn't be more wrong.
>
> Religious journalism is lively, stimulating, vital, and intensely gratifying. It demands the best reporters and the most skillful writers. It serves society in a unique way—literally ennobling it because the produce with which it deals is basically of the soul and the spirit.

By reflecting the thinking of men of goodwill, religious journalism is a potent force in promoting understanding and harmonious relations between all men. . . . What can be more exciting or challenging in journalism than reporting the news of the central force of mankind?

Some Veteran Leaders

On the other hand is a group typified by some of the veteran or now departed religious journalists who have been honored for their work. A few are mentioned to indicate the variety in their backgrounds:

Dr. Dan B. Brummitt, for more than thirty years associated with Methodist journalism, editor of several prominent magazines, and author of many books including novels, learned the hard way: on the job.

Dr. Dan A. Poling, longtime editor of *Christian Herald,* likewise learned while doing, as did Dr. Paul Hutchinson, editor of the *Christian Century;* Professor Harold A. Ehrensperger, first editor of *motive* and an author of fiction and nonfiction books; Bishop T. Otto Nall, who went to the United Methodist episcopate from editorship of *The Christian Advocate;* Dr. James DeForest Murch, founder of several Disciples of Christ publications and onetime editor and manager of *United Evangelical Action;* Francis D. Nichol, editor of the Seventh-day Adventist *Review and Herald;* Dr. George Walker Buckner, editor of *World Call;* Dr. Benjamin P. Browne, for many years editorial executive of the Christian Board of Publications of the American Baptist Churches and editor of *Baptist Leader;* Father Robert C. Hartnett, editor of *America,* a leading Catholic weekly; and Dr. William B. Lipphard, editor of *Missions* and secretary of the Associated Church Press.

Whichever path they followed, these persons and the hundreds of others on religious publications staffs and the personnel rosters of agencies and broadcasting offices work in essentially the same manner and with the same materials as secular journalists.

This fact is the strength of the example of the *Christian Science Monitor* and the other church-sponsored dailies published in this country, the Salt Lake City *Deseret News*, published by the Mormons, and *The News World*, issued by the Moon group. The sponsors of the *Monitor* have made it a high-quality, influential paper known all over the world. Foreign readers and even many in the United States often forget that it is published by a religious body despite its revealing name, but they are cognizant of its high ideals and standards. It should be noted that the *Monitor* is unusual in religious journalism, for it is not a newspaper about religion as is the weekly, the *National Courier*. It is a standard, international daily, recently changed to tabloid format, with strong emphasis on news interpretation and is devoid of most of the trivia so characteristic of the commercial newspapers. Chiefly, however, it de-emphasizes the sordid, never sensationalizing for the sake of sales and advertising, a policy barely appreciated by the public. The *Monitor* is intended as an example of religion in practice. Members of other faiths than Christian Science may dispute that denomination's beliefs and procedures at some points, but they cannot deny the high standards set by the paper, which few other religious publications have attempted.

The *Deseret News* is a more conventional type of publication, with its own record of accomplishments on the local scene.

Religious and Secular Communications Differ

The differences between religious and secular communications should be recognized clearly, for vocationally they are significant. They fall into six groups:

1. The religious communicator must possess a special vocabulary. It is different for Episcopal writers and editors than for Wesleyan Methodists, for those who work with the Mormons, and those with Roman Catholics or one of the Jewish groups. Like sociology, engineering, or medicine, religion has its special language, its argot. Added to the hundreds of such obvious widely used terms as *sacrament, altar,* and *vestment* are particularized words by the score: *phylacteries, jube, pyx, urceole,* and *euchology* are but a few.

2. The religious communicator, especially if he be in reality a "pencil pusher" trying to clarify what others have written or said, must have the patience and understanding to translate the technical writing of theologians so that John C. Churchgoer can understand it. The journalist must battle against religious and theological obscurities. Plain English must replace a sentence like this: "Ethical monotheism supplies that which pantheism misses." The journalist must read and reread until he can understand such assertions: "In other words, if we are to get far in the development of personalism, we have to build on a system that we can—for purposes of our daily experience at least—regard as impersonal—some fixities with laws with which we can deal without explaining anything to them, or apologizing to them (if I may be pardoned so grotesque a phrasing)."

And if rereading does not bring understanding, the religious journalist must either write to the author for

BIOGRAPHICAL BACKGROUND

Self-taught Journalist Edits Church Newspaper

One day in 1976 the author of this book received copies of various religious publications for examination before helping to lead a workshop for their editors and other staff.

A few of the newspapers and magazines issued by the several denominations represented stood out as superior in one way or another: typographically, as news conveyors, or in the forthrightness and timeliness of their editorials.

One of the newsiest, best-presented graphically, firmest in editorial opinion, and broadest in function was *The Virginia Churchman,* published in Richmond.

At the workshop, later, the person responsible for this excellent state paper, which is issued under the authority of the Episcopal Diocese of Virginia but is independent, turned out to be Benjamin P. Campbell. Later investigation turned up the fact that Ben Campbell, as he usually is called and signs himself, has a background that makes him a more or less self-taught religious journalist. He is aided by a staff of three on this paper of 25,000 circulation.

Now in his mid-thirties, Ben Campbell has been an Episcopalian since his birth in Washington, D.C. He went to school in Arlington, Virginia, then went to Williams College for his BA. There he worked three years on the college paper, first as a reporter and later as executive editor. He received, as do many college editors, only what he calls "peer training."

"My major training," he adds, "was having an English teacher as a mother, and having to write endless research papers all the way through school and in nine years of higher education."

He did have more than print experience, however, because he worked for a year in the Williams radio station, reporting news and announcing. He also helped start a magazine in his final year at college. All alone, since boyhood, he was interested in photography and had studied it a little.

Oxford University in England was next. He attended that world-famous institution for three years on a coveted Rhodes scholarship. In England, he writes, "I was on a major university study committee on student regulations regarding dormitory hours. I found that this kind of research project has been a good background for journalism."

He then attended Virginia Seminary, adding the Master of Divinity degree in 1966. He also reawakened his journalistic interests by helping to found a student newspaper at the seminary.

Ben Campbell came to the *Churchman's* editorship after serving for four years as a parish priest in Lancaster County, Virginia.

"I became familiar there with the issues and concerns of people in a parish," he wrote the author of this book. "I also became familiar with the politics and issues of our particular diocese, and as a regular reader of church publications had formed opinions about what was needed. I served on a major diocesan restructure committee which enabled me to participate in hearings throughout the diocese."

He also read newspapers and magazines and watched television, which familiarized him with the standards and forms of journalism to which people in ordinary society were ordinarily exposed.

"I think this is very important," he wrote, "since this is the market in which we operate. These are the people ... doing the work in our media, and these are the people with whom we compete for time."

But he was not depending on such experiences for the technical skill of newspaper work.

"And for all that," he says, "I would not have believed that I could do a newspaper had I not gone to a career development conference which helped me identify my skills in writing and layout and photography.

"After I took the job I learned to use a darkroom. I

have attended professional seminars and church press workshops to try to keep up to date a little. But I also feel observing what other people are doing—since that is so easy in the publications field — is one of the best ways to learn."

Asked about the necessity of communications, Campbell replied:

"I think that the use and cultivation of modern communications media is one of the most important ministries of the church today. Together with small-group work, counseling, and liturgics it forms a cornerstone of the religious networks of the present and future. Conversely, the neglect of the media by the so-called established denominations is one of the major reasons for their loss of influence, both among their own people and within the society as a whole. I find an exciting tension in my own vocation between the exacting standards of professional journalism and the challenge of my own vocation to serve Christ. The two vocations unite in their commitment to serve truth and to explore what that issue means."

clarification (if it is in typescript) or show the notes to the lecturer (if it is from a speech) and ask for guidance as to meaning. Or ask permission to omit the passage, if not the whole script.

3. The religious communicator, at least after awhile, must know the historical background of the churches and particularly of the denomination in which he or she works. If it is an ecumenical group, the journalist should know the organization's history and personalities as well as its aims and problems. Naturally if such knowledge can be brought to the job, all the better. One can understand why some denominational offices insist on hiring, at least for administrative positions, only persons of their own group. But the employee who begins in a lowly position can learn much of this background while at work. In

fact, many young as well as old persons know little of their denominations' history; an alert young member of the Church of the Brethren who knows where to find the facts and has a retentive mind can speedily learn much about the Moravians, different as they may be in doctrine.

4. The religious journalist or communicator certainly will benefit from having had theological training, but as the examination of the careers in various phases of religious communications shows, not everyone by any means had it. Like communications education, lack of such schooling must in the long run be compensated for in some way. Self-study helps, such as extensive reading of books and periodicals about theology, informal talks with theologians, discussions with competent acquaintances, attendance at classes either at one's own church or at nearby seminaries or college and university religion departments.

Some successful editors and publicists have recommended giving little attention to theology. Since there is no agreement among them, however, and knowledge never is amiss, it would be wise for aspiring persons to make some effort to learn the basics of theology so that they can deal knowledgeably with theological issues and ideas.

Another way to meet the situation is to study theology gradually, if one happens to work in a community providing religious course work, or by obtaining a leave of absence from the job to do the study. As with any other subjects, theology should be followed because the individual is genuinely interested in the facts and ideas, not simply from ambition to add more degrees.

5. The religious communicator must be aware of expectations regarding certain attitudes and types of personal behavior. Such persons are associated, in the public mind, with pastors, rabbis, or missionaries. Some religious journalists are anything but religious. Their work may have been forced upon them (as in the instance of a police reporter who must take the church beat). Even so, it is assumed that they have the conscience and the sense of responsibility to be sincerely religious and to refrain from misconduct.

Religious journalists should no more be expected to act like saints than any other mortals, perhaps. But an attitude toward religion which is hypocritical hardly enables such a journalist to work effectively. When he or she attends a religious meeting where smoking or drinking is considered offensive, respect should be shown for the wishes of the hosts. But self-control should extend to more than these personal choices. It should move the journalist to be fair with facts and ideas in which he or she either has no interest or feels a strong bias.

This special problem is not peculiar to the media but is unusually strong there. On the staff of the religious magazine or in a church news agency office the work requires the same (or a better) code of conduct than that of secular associates. Thus it is easier to be religious as well as a communicator because the atmosphere is conducive. Further, the religious journalist is likely to show greater consideration for the persons being written about. He or she seeks to protect, rather than to exploit, minorities; condescension or looking down is avoided. In preparing articles about missions, for example, the use of dialect is avoided because it tends to perpetuate the weaknesses of people. The reporter refrains from writing about what are sometimes called *natives*, and any sort of discrimination is abhorrent. He or she also refuses to use information told confidentially and off the record. If possible, all off-the-record sessions are avoided. The religious communicator observes something of the spirit of the confessional in all human situations.

6. The attitude of the employer also frequently differs. Although secular offices sometimes hire physically handicapped people or persons suffering from some other difficulty, they are not so likely to do so as the church-sponsored institution, which tends more to think of its obligation to the individuals in society.

A church publisher soon after World War II was asked for a job by a young man fresh from four years' hospital work under Civilian Public Service, the United States government's official provision for conscientious objectors to war. He was hired for three months, and assigned to the denomination's national magazine. After a few days on the job the new editorial assistant found that he had little to do and that actually he was not needed. He began digging up jobs to keep himself busy. Before the end of the three months, staff adjustments resulted in his permanent appointment, and in time he became a top editor.

Some years later he asked his employer, Dr. Roy L. Smith, a noted Methodist editor, author, and columnist, why he had taken him on in the first place.

"I knew that men from CPS would have a difficult time getting jobs," Dr. Smith answered. "I felt that we ought to give you something for a few months so that when you began hunting jobs again you could go from

BIOGRAPHICAL BACKGROUND

A Versatile Communicator—
Writer, Editor, Publicist

Marian W. Groesbeck's career story might just as readily be included in the chapter titled "Publicists of Religion."

For this communicator is so versatile that she writes, edits, and promotes religious materials. She does this work for the Free Methodist Church in the United States, which has its world headquarters at Winona Lake, Indiana, an important center of religious publishing and educational work.

Versatility has been characteristic of Mrs. Groesbeck's life, but the thread that runs through it since her elementary school days has had to do with writing. She also was interested in music, art, sports, and other activities. At Spring Arbor Junior College, in Michigan, she was editor of the newspaper. As a junior she transferred to Greenville College, in Illinois, and there also edited the campus paper, was a member of Scriberus, the writing club, and received her BA *cum laude*. She took courses in bookkeeping, shorthand, and Comptometer operation, among others in

our office rather than directly from CPS, which isn't understood by everyone."

Another young man, whom we also shall leave unnamed, was offered a post as a part-time public relations staffer for a denominational office. Before hiring him, the head of the organization looked over the backgrounds of several candidates. He decided on this applicant, although it was pointed out that the lad was timid, shy, and an unaggressive person for such a position.

"I realize that," was the employer's comment. "I've

the business field. These were eminently useful to her, providing her with what so many arts and communications courses are thought to lack: an understanding of the practical business operations.

Writing promotion for the General Missionary Board of the Free Methodist Church was her first post-college job. That was in 1950. Her school and college journalism experience enabled her to write news and features stories as well as interviews. As time went on the Board office expanded. Mrs. Groesbeck's duties then included planning and promoting motion picture films, planning and executing annual reports, taking photographs, producing newsletters, brochures, and other printed pieces, and raising funds. When she began this work one person was on the staff. It grew to six.

Sensing the need for more skills, Mrs. Groesbeck meanwhile had taken advertising, graphic arts, and feature writing courses. In 1969 there came an interruption. Her husband, Walter, was made director of the Paul Carlson Foundation in Chicago, so they moved to that city. With the foundation needing funding, Mrs. Groesbeck took over its public relations and fundraising. She produced a newsletter, news stories, spoke at meetings, prepared proposals to foundations, wrote direct mail copy, and planned fundraising campaigns.

When the Free Methodist

heard him speak in public and I've seen that he's weak on some things that a good public relations man ought to know. But with a little coaching and advising he'll gain confidence and will learn to do a good job.

"I think we must do something for him, help to bring him out and help him to overcome his reticence. Our job is not such a high-speed one, anyway."

Laurence Hosie, while executive secretary of the Council of Churches of Indianapolis, Indiana, declared that he thought all ministers should have religious

Church formed a new office at Winona Lake in 1971 called Information and Stewardship, Mrs. Groesbeck was named assistant to the director. Among this office's responsibilities were the entire fund-raising, promotional, and information programs for the whole denomination. At the same time her husband became executive assistant to the missionary secretary, having been a former missionary himself.

"We did not call our work 'fund raising,'" Mrs. Groesbeck explains. "We did not think of the work as that. I did not. I wanted to be a channel of information and interpretation so that people would have the opportunity to participate in many ways—through their concern, interest, prayer, volunteer service, and giving of their time and money.... Our concern is for people, rather than programs."

The shift to magazine editing came in 1975, when Mrs. Groesbeck was named editor of *Missionary Tidings*, published by the Women's Missionary Society. As this sketch is being written, she is entirely responsible for the magazine's purposes, design, layout, many of the features, subscriptions, editing, and other areas. As with so many church periodicals, the editor must be versatile and capable of doing all the work connected with issuing it except production. Assisting Mrs. Groesbeck are a circulation worker full time and a half-time editorial assistant. Some copy comes from missionaries and nations in the field; art copy is bought from free-lancers.

Since 1968 Mrs. Groesbeck, as part of her work, has visited the missions abroad around the world. Her husband leads tours to the mission centers and she accompanies him as co- or assistant director.

---

journalism training because it would make them better critics of what is being done by the church. He did not expect that all church persons would necessarily need to be trained religious journalists because they study it, but if they understood what is needed they can advise and guide others who are professionals.

Here again we have the concept of an activity doing something for the life of the individual as well as for the institution he or she serves. Such a concept is more likely to be held by the staffs of institutions in religious communications than by those in other specialties.

What One Person Accomplished

What can be accomplished is illustrated by the career of Everett C. Parker, a pioneer in religious broadcasting in the United States.

Parker was known in the field for his work with the Protestant Radio Commission, later called the Broadcasting and Film Commission of the National Council of Churches of Christ, and the similarly named commission of the Churches of Christ in the U.S.A. He also helped bring religious radio and television into greater prominence by his coauthorship of *Religious Radio* and his authorship of a later volume, *Religious Television,* as well as by his direction of various workshops in many areas. These seminars were for religious leaders wishing to use the best techniques in presenting different types of religious broadcasts. In 1954 Mr. Parker broadened his influence by becoming director of the central communications office of the then Congregational Christian Church. He now is director of the office of communication, United Church of Christ.

While still in high school in Chicago, his birthplace, Parker settled on his career specialty. He produced a series of radio programs about city high school teachers. His professional radio work for Station WCFL in

Chicago began right after he left school. His interest in broadcasting continued when he went to the University of Chicago, but now was coupled with publicity, for he worked in the university's publicity office as well as for the nationally popular "Round Table" program. Both types of work helped determine his lifelong professional interests.

A year after graduation Parker was named assistant chief of radio for the Works Progress Administration (WPA), producing network and recorded programs for national distribution. In another venture he ran a public relations and advertising agency. From WPA he went to New Orleans to manage a radio station, WJBW, and then entered his religious broadcasting career with the Protestant Radio Commission. In the meantime he studied at Chicago Theological Seminary, earning his degree *magna cum laude*.

Parker's connections with electronic communication mounted rapidly thereafter. He was organizer and head of an interdenominational Protestant broadcasting group, the Joint Religious Radio Commission. For twelve years he was a lecturer in communication at Yale Divinity School and for six he headed the Communications Research Project sponsored by Yale and the National Council of Churches.

That he can write as well as broadcast is evident from other activities. He has been a correspondent for *The Christian Century*, serving also as an editor-at-large from 1963 to 1971. He so far has added two books to those already mentioned. They are *The Television-Radio Audience and Religion* and *Television-Radio-Film for Churchmen* (coauthored). As producer and director of national television programs he has to his credit *Off to Adventure*, a series, and *Bible Puppets*. As a motion picture producer he was responsible for *The Pumpkin Coach* and other films.

Dr. Parker's awards are numerous: the Alfred I. Du Pont—Columbia University Award for public service in broadcasting and the American Jewish Committee's Human Relations award are among them.

His contribution so far, as described by his denomination, has been "to make broadcasting accountable to the public, and to insure access to the air to blacks, other minorities, and women." An example is a program called *Check Your Local Stations*, begun in 1974. It "prepares community leaders to evaluate the performance of radio and television stations and to present ideas for improved service to station managements." Parker also launched another project: Communications Recruitment and Training, Inc., described as "a career awareness program which introduces minority high school students to the business and other off-the-air jobs in broadcasting."

Perhaps he is best known for his battles for fair treatment of black people by broadcasting stations in the 1960s. The United Church of Christ in 1964 filed a petition against WLBT-TV, a Jackson, Mississippi, station, to deny its license renewal "because it discriminated against blacks." When the Federal Communications Commission granted a conditional renewal it was appealed by the denomination. This resulted in what has been considered in the industry a landmark decision written by Judge Warren Burger, then on the Circuit Court and later Justice of the United States Supreme Court. It granted members of the public "the right to intervene in license renewal proceedings of the FCC and ordered the Commission to hear the charges being made by the Office of Communication" of the church.

But that was not the end. The FCC refused to act against the station. Justice Burger, making a second significant decision, then revoked the station's license. This was the first time a station was punished for not obeying the act that says it must serve, in the familiar clause, "the public interest, convenience, or necessity."

Other cases followed, many of them settled without recourse to the law. Another widely publicized one occurred in Texarkana, Texas. Black citizens filed a petition to deny license renewal to station KTAL-TV because it, too, failed to provide broadcasts needed by the community. Parker's office assisted, and KTAL signed a contract with a dozen local organizations pledging "improved television service to the entire area."

Parker began on a secular job but after a time moved into the religious setting, reaching a position of socially significant power to carry out the ideals of his religion, but within the church.

For further reading about being on the religious job:

BOOKS

Dorothy Day, *The Long Loneliness.* New York: Harper, 1952.

John Gill, *Tide Without Turning: Elijah P. Lovejoy and Freedom of the Press.* Boston: Starr King Press, 1958.

E. C. Routh, *Adventures in Christian Journalism.* Nashville: Broadman Press, 1951.

Bengt K. D. Simonsson, *The Way of the Word*. London: United Society for Christian Literature, 1965.

W. Bertrand Stevens, *Editor's Quest*. New York: Morehouse-Gorham, 1940.

Roland E. Wolseley, ed., *Writing for the Religious Market*. New York: Association Press, 1956.

ARTICLES

James W. Carty, Jr., "Christian Communication Careers." *The Link*, August, 1961.

John Cogley, "Farewell to Father Gillis." *Commonweal*, April 5, 1957.

James M. Flanagan, "The Man and His Task." *The Christian Evangelist*, June 23, 1958.

Martin E. Marty, "How It Looks in the Moonlight." *The Christian Century*, November 3, 1976.

T. Otto Nall, "Good News Is His Business." *Christian Advocate*, September 20, 1956.

"Paul Hutchinson," *The Christian Century*, April 25, 1956. Also see "Happy Man," *Time*, April 23, 1956.

Theo E. Sommerkamp, "Christian Journalism: A Worthy Field." *Brotherhood Journal*, April-June, 1957.

6 Publicists of Religion

Most cities have at least one church or temple that is so busy it is in the news constantly. New members join steadily. Soon a large wing must be added; it is used to serve the whole community as well as the congregation. Its church school flourishes.

For each institution like this one, every community also has one or more that merely struggle along, unknown and unheard of except by a few loyal parishioners and the neighbors. Most members remain out of habit or denominational loyalty. From half to a third of the pews are empty on Sundays. The pastor is discouraged; the parsonage run down. The congregation meets in a gloomy setting and has difficulty finding teachers and choir members. The church does little for its community or for the world at large; it barely keeps going.

Publicists of Religion

If one looks into what makes the first type of church progress, one generally finds an enthusiastic and well-organized leadership to which an alert and active laity responds. The church, by having a dynamic program, has attracted hardworking persons who want to be part of a useful religious enterprise.

One also learns that usually such a church organization knows how to publicize itself. It does so by using a professional public relations firm's services (sometimes donated) or by organizing a public relations committee consisting of members experienced in public relations, journalism, publicity, advertising, or some other aspect of communications. Whichever method is used, the persons doing the work cooperate with the media locally to keep each other and the community informed about the church. And, contrariwise, the dull, languishing church usually has not made much use of printing, advertising, posters, and other devices to tell its story. Nor does it have much of a story to tell.

Publicity and public relations programs alone cannot turn a decaying church into a living one. A living spirit must be there first. But such programs can help put more life into the church.

Public relations, publicity, promotion, and press agentry, four related but not identical activities, now are accepted techniques. The first three are employed in many churches. Large and small denominations alike have offices for such work, which is done as well on the local scene by more and more community institutions. Estimates of the number of public relations workers indicate that they are in the hundreds of thousands, serving business, industry, government, education, and every other human enterprise. How many are in religious work is not recorded. But almost all types of religious enterprises now engage people for such work, an indication of its mounting importance.

Public information and *public communications* are terms used in place of *public relations* because of the abuse by some secular publicists of these techniques. A public relations officer, a public information officer, and a director of communications perform similar duties.

Communications and Public Relations

Religious publicists use all the techniques of communications, including the related fields. Knowledge of mass communications, especially writing, is needed for a position of consequence in public relations.

Although they may sound alike, public relations, publicity, promotion, and press agentry are not synonyms. All are propaganda activities rather than strictly objective communications work.

Public relations is concerned with influencing attitudes. Irving S. Olds, a businessman, defined it as the creation and carrying out of broad policies that will be reflected in favorable public opinion. Others have defined it as doing good and getting credit for it or as the science of attitude control. Religious people do not worry about the credit but they want the good to be accomplished and to be known for its example.

Publicity uses the means of communication with all people or with some specific public. Its aim is to convey facts and opinions in ways that will publicize those facts and opinions as widely as possible. It is a tool of public relations.

Promotion is any activity intended to attract a public for the purposes of business transaction, such as a sale. It, too, is a public relations tool.

Press agentry is work done by people who have many of the same purposes as those who use the other three tools, with the connotation of using stunts or sensationalism to obtain attention. Circuses can use press agents more appropriately than can churches. But it, also, is a public relations tool.

Thus an essential difference between public relations and the others is that public relations workers do not necessarily write, edit, advertise, speak in public, and do anything educational or journalistic to carry out their duties, although most do one of these as part of their work. They do so because only the largest organizations can employ specialists for each activity. Public relations experts must understand the institutions they serve and act as counselors on policy. Big public relations offices include publicity writers, advertising copywriters, artists, photographers, article and feature writers, film and broadcasting script writers, and promotion people.

But those persons in charge are skilled in far different activities. Theirs are the areas of human relations, of labor-management affairs, parent-teacher-pupil conflict, pastor-congregation relations, or other group relationships. They are—or should be—acquainted with the findings of modern psychology. They are problem solvers but, what is more important, they attempt to prevent the occurrence of problems.

Combining These Activities

All institutions of religion combine these four propa-

BIOGRAPHICAL BACKGROUND

Religious Newsman, Magazine Staffer, and Then Publicist

If George M. Daniels has an important post as a publicist in the United Methodist Church it may be because he has done everything that could prepare him for his duties as director of Interpretative Services of his denomination's Board of Global Ministries.

Here were his steps:

He obtained a bachelor of journalism degree at Drake University and then went on to add the master of science in the same subject, but this time at the Graduate School of Journalism of Columbia University.

Then he went into the journalistic field as a writer for the Associated Negro Press, a news agency with headquarters in Chicago, remaining for a year. That experience in the early 1950s may have begun an interest in African affairs that was to become strong fifteen years later. The ANP, the largest black news gathering agency ever to function in the United States, gave much attention to African news and served many black publications which would have had difficulty obtaining news of that continent otherwise.

From the ANP Mr. Daniels went to the editorial rooms of another prominent Chicago journalistic institution—the Chicago *Daily Defender*, for many years one of the few black dailies in the country and since early in this century a leading newspaper, now the flagship publication of the Sengstacke Newspapers, a group with units in several cities. At the *Defender* he was a reporter and feature writer.

After five years he entered religious communications at *Together*, then a nationally distributed United Methodist monthly of consumer magazine quality with a circulation close to one million. He wrote news and feature material for it as well as for *The Christian Advocate*, another Methodist

> magazine, from 1957 to 1961.
>
> Then came the shift to public relations, his present work. It came in that last year, 1961, when he moved to the Board of Global Ministries in New York, with the title of associate news director and was responsible for an area in which he had had rich experience: news work. To that he added public relations duties. Seven years later he was named to the position he held in 1977.
>
> Since his work with the Board, Daniels has become a specialist in African and Caribbean affairs. He has traveled widely in Africa, the West Indies, Central and South America, and written about them for United States and Caribbean periodicals.
>
> He is author of *The Church in New Nations* and has edited three other books, each dealing with areas of Africa. In 1976 he published *Black College Guide and Handbook.*
>
> Among the several awards he has won was the $3,000 fellowship in journalism named for Ralph Stoody, the church publicist whose career story also appears in this chapter. The Chicago Newspaper Guild's Front Page Award went to him while he was on the *Defender* for "outstanding performance in the field of journalism." He also won the Windy City Press Club Award for general reporting and the Robert E. Sherwood Award for travel and study in Latin America.

ganda activities or concentrate on one or two, for merely to exist is to have some sort of public relations, good or bad. The world of religion is made up of many publics; everything done by any institution within that world will reach one or more of those publics: the members, the church staff, the community, the regional organization, the denomination through the world, the outsiders.

A modest example of public relations at work might be the office of an overseas mission board of almost any Protestant denomination. It is responsible for the production of booklets, leaflets, brochures, pamphlets, newsletters, and other small pieces of printed matter about the mission enterprise supported by the denomination. It oversees preparing photographs, films, filmstrips, cassettes, and other materials. Also, it arranges for returning missionaries or newsworthy members from overseas to be interviewed by newspapers, magazines, and broadcasting stations. Out of its offices go news releases and offers of illustrations to church and secular publications informing them about events of public interest. It publishes a magazine with a world circulation, perhaps, of one hundred thousand copies monthly.

All this and much more is done to foster broader understanding and awareness of the mission activities. It is intended, also, to produce favorable reaction to the work and greater support for it. All these journalistic and other communications tools are put to the task of influencing the attitudes of the various publics surrounding the denomination.

Why Churches Publicize

Why must the religious bodies supply the media with material in these ways? Should not the newspapers, magazines, and other media seek this information themselves? They should. But it is impossible for a single medium to go to each religious news source in so complex and enormous a society as exists in a modern nation.

In a city of three hundred thousand, for example, there may be as many as one hundred and fifty churches and temples. Just to telephone each regularly, much less visit the persons in charge at each, would consume the entire time of several reporters. That same newspaper must obtain the news, as well, of the business, sports, club, school, and all the other worlds about it. A city's organizations, therefore, must cooperate (and to some extent compete for space and time) with the media if they are to be represented. This situation explains why a skillful and cooperative public relations person in a local church is able to obtain more attention than others.

George E. Sweazy in *Effective Evangelism* tells about Oscar Wilde's Aunt Jane, who died of mortification when no one came to her grand ball. She died without knowing she had failed to mail the invitations. "That," Dr. Sweazy observes, "is the story of many a fine church which has wonderful worship services, a splendid program—has everything, in fact, save a way of making some connection with those outside, who always assume that what the church has is for someone else."

Through publicity and public relations work the modern church can avoid "Aunt Jane's" mistake. It can profit from exposure on the intricate, complex communications systems and make its mark in spite of the great competition between media for the attention of readers, listeners, and viewers. The church's good deeds will be less effective in proportion to the degree to which they are left hidden.

The Seventh-day Adventists, with a membership of only around 465,000 (there are about 48,000,000 Catholics in the United States and around 12,000,000 Southern Baptists) are far more widely known in proportion to their size because of capable use of public relations techniques. They were among the first to set up a news bureau to acquaint the press with the work of the denomination. They have a Department of Public Affairs in Washington, D.C., and several regional news bureaus. J. K. Ferren, for many years head of the original news bureau, was a leader in impressing upon the Adventists that their church should do something about preparing young men and women of education and talent for careers of responsibility in the press and related fields. This denomination is known, also, for its excellent periodicals. These serve the constituents as well as the unchurched public. It also has led in preparation of church publicity guides, including films for stimulating interest in publicizing the local church.

Becoming a Publicist

How does one become a publicist for the church? The careers of a few of the better known pioneer church publicists are a guide.

That of Ralph Stoody, until his retirement executive director of the Commission on Public Information (then known familiarly as Methodist Information) of the United Methodist Church, shows one of the paths that a person might follow in the religious public relations and publicity field.

Stoody went to college and seminary at Ohio Wesleyan University, Boston University School of Theology, and Gordon College of Theology and Missions. To the BA, STB., and STD. degrees he added graduate study at Garrett Theological Seminary, Columbia University, and Harvard University. While at Gordon, Stoody made a major contribution to religious journalism: his dissertation, entitled *Religious Journalism: Whence and Whither?* Completed in 1939, it is one of the few attempts to bring together historical facts

BIOGRAPHICAL BACKGROUND

The Nun Who Is Writer as Well as Publicist

Nuns, traditionally, do not aspire to careers in the ordinary sense. They are granted freedom from certain concerns and responsibilities, but they acquire others in exchange. They are expected not to seek financial profits from their labors and to live lives of service to God and society.

An example of what can be accomplished by such a sister, despite many demands upon her time and energy, is provided by Sister Anne Paye, RSM, of the College of Misericordia, in Dallas, Pennsylvania. Religion is at the center of her life as teacher, writer, and publicist. She is a member of the Sisters of Mercy order.

Like thousands of other girls, Sister Anne worked on her high school and college papers as reporter and editor. Until she studied for her PhD at Syracuse University she had majored in English, but had to her credit a college reporting course. To that she added a newspaper program and for her dissertation wrote a study of science journalism and science journalists. In the course on religious writing at S.U. she became one of the only two students ever to publish all the work done in the class, which by this writing has been offered for 23 years.

Sister Anne's publications out of that class included an editorial on civil rights for *The Nation;* an article on the personality cult of the president for the same magazine (it was reprinted in *U.S. News and World Report* and summarized in *Time* magazine); an article for *Ave Maria* magazine about Father John Lynch, the poet; and others for *Today* and *Catholic School Journal.* Nor was that all. Her short story was placed in *Lamp* and some newspaper pieces appeared in diocesan and secular publications.

She returned to Dallas to

serve for four years as director of publicity for Misericordia. At the same time she was one of five Sisters of Mercy who comprised a Beyond Prejudice Team. The members spoke on the racial issue to various audiences. During 1969-1970 Sister Anne was consultant at the Educational TV Studio, Rockville Center, New York, diocese of the Catholic Church. The area of specialty was black studies. Produced was a series of history lessons for eighth-graders. Entitled "400 Years," it reviewed the history of the Black race in this country.

Beginning in 1971 she returned to public relations work as director of Mercy Information Center in Dallas, which she describes as the public relations arm of her order in the province of Scranton, Pennsylvania. It is, she explains, "involved principally in publicity, brochures, program."

In 1976 she published *Heritage of Faith*, a history of the Sisters of Mercy from 1874 to 1975, her major piece of writing in recent years.

Sister Anne Paye's work in the mid-1970s has been accomplished despite the fact that a long illness has made her stints at the typewriter not as easy to perform as they once were.

and evaluations of religious journalism and has been a source for graduate students and writers ever since.

In the years between attending the School of Theology at Boston and becoming director of his denomination's public information bureau, Stoody held pastorates in Vermont, Maine, and Massachusetts. While serving as a minister he was a correspondent and feature writer for several large secular newspapers. His full-time journalistic work began when he became an editorial associate on *The Epworth Herald,* a young people's magazine.

In the years that followed he contributed to numerous religious periodicals; served briefly as a war correspondent for Religious News Service during World War II in the Mediterranean and North African theaters; edited the *Daily Christian Advocate* for a Methodist General Conference in 1938; had charge of press relations for the World Methodist Conference in Oxford, England, in 1951; and was press aide to Bishop W. C. Martin, president of the National Council of Churches, in a visit to Japan and Korea in 1953-54.

The quadrennial reports of the work of the organization then known as Methodist Information, with a half-dozen branch offices in several cities, have been an impressive collection of statistics about the many operations of the office. Stoody did especially effective work not only in developing the system and cooperating with the public relations officers of the various areas of the denomination but also in setting up seminars in publicity for pastors, helping them with their press and broadcasting procedures.

Old-time secular newsmen, often given to looking skeptically at religious journalists and publicists, always spoke of Ralph Stoody, when he was head of MI, as one of their own kind, one who "knew his stuff." They discerned in him understanding of the problems faced by print and electronic media journalists. He followed the philosophy not of space-grabbing, but of running a news-dissemination office that cooperated with the media, relying on facts rather than on opinions and seeking no special treatment. Much of his experience went into his book, *A Handbook of Church Public Relations.*

When he was retired in 1964 he was succeeded by Arthur West, who came to the position from public relations and journalism work at Northwestern University and the University of Chicago. He had been head of the Chicago office of Methodist Information from 1948 to his assumption of the executive directorship.

The complexity of the duties of such an administrator in the later 1970s can be illustrated by a brief account of how a general conference of the denomination is publicized. The example used is the session (held every four years by the United Methodists) held in 1976 in Portland, Oregon. Beyond preparation of the conventional press books and news releases and pictures ordinarily provided, the following were done:

A set of five audio-cassette tapes and a 20-piece slide set, called Newscope Sight-Sound Reports, were made available to the church membership. These brought "the sights and sounds of the General Conference, plus an interpretation of the actions, to every local church." Floyd Kalber, an NBC broadcaster, narrated two of the cassettes. One cassette was released two weeks before the sessions and discussed the principal issues coming before the assembly. The second, third, and fourth cassettes were issued from Portland and gave their users the addresses, debates, and interviews with key persons in the meetings. The final cassette, to be used with the slides, summarized the legal actions.

Newscope Newsletter, a weekly publication of the church, produced a special news packet consisting of a dozen issues on the conference alone. Like the cassettes it reported on the conference before, during and afterwards. As had been done many times before, a *Daily Christian Advocate* was published, giving complete reports on all documents, debates, discussions, and final outcomes.

Gordon R. Lindsey, left, director of press relations for the American Bible Society, is shown with Clifford P. Macdonald, managing editor of the society's monthly magazine, American Bible Society Record. (Photo courtesy American Bible Society)

An unusual and new step was Infoserv, a toll-free telephone information service for leaders of the church. It offered a recorded report on conference actions. It was available for 3-minute periods between 4:00 p.m. and 8:00 a.m. during the sessions at Portland.

John L. Fortson, another publicist, who after working as a newspaper editor, a Washington writer for United Press International, and in the New York offices of N.W. Ayer & Son, one of the largest advertising agencies, was named director of public relations for the National Council of Churches.

Donald Bolles, one of Mr. Fortson's successors, attended neither a theological school nor a college. He prepared for his post in religious public relations by learning on the journalistic job. He had been on a country weekly, a small-town daily, and with a large wire service, the Associated Press. He entered the public relations field with an agency that had corporation and association accounts, then shifted to the National Council.

Because of his background, Mr. Bolles said, "I do not feel very dogmatic about what it takes to be a religious journalist." He added:

"I think that the chief elements in being able to interpret the Christian cause to Christians are writing ability, sympathy with the Christian cause, and a large amount of understanding of people. Personally, I am inclined to believe that an ability to be objective is a prerequisite to being a good editor. It could be argued that some become so thoroughly immersed in theology that their objectivity is impaired."

It would take a much longer book to tell the stories of Stanley I. Stuber, Woodrow A. Geier, Roland S. Gammon, Albert McClellan, C. E. Bryant, Erik W. Modean, and other men and women who have labored for many different groups in a relatively new occupation.

A New Occupation

Public relations is new in the history of communications. All other phases of religious communications work except broadcasting are older than public relations and its subordinate activities. It was not until early in this century that business and industry, the first to use this activity in the modern sense, realized that they must have favorable public opinion. Before the advent of public relations counsels like Ivy L. Lee and Edward L. Bernays, an institution began worrying over its reputation (or to use the present-day expression, its "image") only after it was in trouble with a public—internal or external.

The world of religion has been slower to awaken to the need for better understanding and to the contribution that communications and related fields can make to that understanding. Today the larger denominations and many of the smaller ones, and the subdivisions of each, have public relations offices. They engage beginners as editorial assistants to write news, edit copy, plan advertising, and other such duties, and they occasionally call for candidates of rich experience to fill major positions.

Public relations has developed slowly as an occupation within the church because it is abused in some areas, such as the entertainment and business worlds, where at times it is used to misrepresent rather than interpret the sponsors or to cover up malfeasance of some sort. Also it is difficult to measure results. How, for example, can the Seventh-day Adventist Church measure the effectiveness of its efforts in correcting public confusion of that denomination with the Seventh-day Baptists or the Advent Christian Church, two others of like-sounding names?

Techniques have been developed to attempt such measurements; in small, controlled experiments it is possible. The religious communicator who enters this type of work therefore must know how to solve such problems. Public relations offices use all the communications tools and expect staff members to be acquainted with and skilled in use of such tools. The best-fitted persons also bring knowledge of social psychology, behavioral sciences, and propaganda methods.

Because of this difficulty in measuring results, sometimes it is difficult to obtain cooperation from an unprepared constituency and of church leaders not convinced that a planned public relations program is needed. This problem reveals itself at all levels within the church, from the instance of a board that does not wish to release information about its workings all the way to a local pastor or rabbi who, fearful of being called a publicity seeker, refuses even to provide local news media with a photograph.

Yet the church needs to carry its message to the people inside and outside its own circle. The press is only one of many avenues. But there are too many churches and too few persons trained in professional communications to grasp this message and present it with understanding. Through public relations work, therefore, the church assists the media. For it the church needs men and women who understand religion, the church, and the media and who possess the skills and training that will put these media to work to tell religion's story.

More information is to be found in:

BOOKS

W. Austin Brodie, *Keeping Your Church in the News.* New York: Revell, 1962.

Allen H. Center, *Public Relations Practices—Case Studies.* Englewood Cliffs, N.J.: Prentice-Hall, 1975.

Edward L. Greif, *The Silent Pulpit.* New York: Holt, Rinehart & Winston, 1964.

Philip A. Johnson, Norman Temme, and Charles C. Hushaw, *Telling the Good News.* St. Louis: Concordia, 1962.

Raymond G. Mecca, *Your Church Is News.* Valley Forge, Pa.: Judson Press, 1975.

Lawrence W. Nolte, *Fundamentals of Public Relations.* New York: Pergamon Press, 1974.

Raymond Simon, ed., *Perspectives in Public Relations.* Norman: University of Oklahoma Press, 1966.

Roland E. Wolseley, *Interpreting the Church Through Press and Radio.* Philadelphia: Muhlenberg Press, 1951.

7 The Missionary Communicators

Missionary communicators do some of the most dramatic, difficult, and rewarding work in the world of religion. They combine the experience and responsibilities of the missionary with the skills of the writer, editor, broadcaster, photographer, artist, or graphic artist and the techniques of the specially-trained educator. Sometimes these hardworking and gifted people join several of these abilities and duties.

Young people are attracted to such work because of its usefulness; older persons also have been known to give up their secular jobs and practice a new vocation of this type in foreign fields. They go not necessarily as evangelists but as bringers of practical knowledge. They prepare materials for new literates and conduct workshops of religious writers and editors on most

The Missionary Communicatiors 137

continents. They guide the managers of newspapers and magazines of religion, the publishers of books of religion, the makers of films in a missions setting.

One such person, a young woman named Ruth Eshenaur, is in Nairobi, Kenya, Africa, as this book is being prepared. Her story, in its general outlines, is typical. When Dr. Eshenaur (she holds a PhD in communications) was working for her master's degree in a large university school of journalism she left tracts on the chairs of her classrooms. Or she dropped small stacks of the leaflets near stairways. Most of her fellow students were not used to such zeal about religion. About a rock concert, yes. But religion. . . .

So the young evangelist became somewhat conspicuous. She saw no reason why, if other students could distribute leaflets for lectures and political meetings of one sort or another, she should not spend some time spreading the gospel. And in print.

The attitude toward Ruth Eshenaur's evangelistic fervor was typical of the experience some religious young people encounter in schools and colleges populated mainly by students not committed to their religion in her particular way.

But the reaction only spurred her on, for obviously it was all the more necessary to communicate what she stood for to these unsaved souls. Was this not a basic tenet of religious communication: to spread the good word of salvation?

In time Miss Eshenaur was in a position to communicate her message in a bigger way. But we should start at the beginning.

Although a West Virginian by birth, she does not

sound like one, if she ever did, her speech having been internationalized by now. Since Americans with strong accents often confuse the peoples of other countries, that is just as well.

She has both training and practical experience in communications. Her degrees are from four institutions—a bachelor of theology from Detroit Bible College, a bachelor of arts from Marshall University, a master of arts in journalism from Syracuse University, and a doctor of philosophy in communications from Southern Illinois University. She also has studied at Marietta and Wheaton Colleges.

Miss Eshenaur edited the yearbook at Detroit Bible College, and that year's issue won a first-class honor rating from the Associated Collegiate Press. She has been associate editor of *Impact*, a magazine published by the Conservative Baptist Foreign Missionary Society. It, too, won honors during her service there, this time from the Associated Church Press.

Her articles have appeared in *Journalism Quarterly*, *Grass Roots Editor*, and other periodicals, including the religious press.

Perhaps her greatest contribution thus far has been made through the work she was doing in the mid-1970s. She was, as she is as this is being written, a member of the faculty of the International Institute of Communications in Nairobi, which she joined in 1975. The Institute is a project of Daystar Communications, which is described in its prospectus as "a group of specialists in research, development, and training for effective Christian communication."

Daystar provides "a consultation service for churches

Dr. Ruth Eshenaur of the faculty of the International Institute of Christian Communications, Nairobi, here is showing Johnson Okolo, an IICC student, how to write Christian literature for Luhya people in Kenya.

and missions which couples wide experience with contemporary techniques of analysis, measurement, and evaluation," the staff explains.

Dr. Eshenaur is one of twelve faculty members, but she does more than teach writing courses or guide the students in mass communications research methods. She does public relations work, writes lesson plans, prepares catalogs and other printed matter; for a time she produced the monthly *Daystar Reports*. She takes pictures as well as writes. She edits some of these materials and does charcoal sketches to illustrate them.

"I also," she wrote in a newsletter, "have been learning Swahili . . . and teaching Sunday school. . . . Ideally it would help if I knew scores of African languages . . . because we get students from all over Africa, many of whom don't know English well. This creates problems

. . . since English is the language of instruction."

Looking back on her education and training, this busy missionary communicator wrote in 1976 that she wishes she "had been able to write a dissertation which would have prepared me better for what I am doing now, such as a study to develop a curriculum (including self-teaching materials) for training Christian writers, journalists, publishers, broadcasters, communicators in the Third World and a curriculum on how to update missionaries in these areas. I should have taken more courses in international journalism, public relations, Christian education (I'm getting into that area some here), management, and spoken French. I need more experience in these areas and in writing for electronic media, editing, publishing, and distribution in the Third World."

Early in 1977 Ruth was assigned to write Christian education materials and to train writers for the African Inland Church, after attending language school.

Clearly, her work is arduous, as has been true of all types of missionary effort for many years. But she has a strong sense of mission and duty, for she adds to all this prayer and Bible group leadership. Her membership is in the Nairobi Baptist Church. There she teaches Sunday school and does other church work. She has been a Baptist all her life, working with whichever wing of it had a congregation where she was studying or working professionally.

A full record of her activities—literature distribution, street meetings, conducting teacher training classes, directing vacation Bible schools, working with groups on campuses, visiting jails, leading Bible study and prayer groups, for example, would be far too long to include here. But she is a hardworking communicator with the zeal that helps her to face the strains and hardships of her occupation.

Religious Communications for Missionaries
In one of Dr. Frank Laubach's earliest books he wrote:

> One contribution not yet made by any college in India is called for at the present juncture. That is the establishment of a school of journalism for the new literature written with restricted word lists. Students who show particular genius in using simple words while they are in the lower grades should be given special scholarships to such schools. . . . With the present great literacy campaign upon us there will be need of several such schools and of thousands of graduate journalists in the immediate future.[1]

That statement was published in India in 1940. Almost a decade later, Dr. Laubach went to Syracuse University to propose that its School of Journalism offer courses that would help prepare young people produce such materials for new literates. He called it simple journalism, but until then his idea had been of no interest at several other institutions. The late dean, Dr. M. Lyle Spencer, who was a minister's son, saw that Syracuse had a responsibility in the plan.

Soon the faculty was presented with a proposal. A program in religious journalism, using the core offerings of the school as its base, was ready for students by fall of 1949. A handful comprised the first group. One was from India, another from British Guiana, the rest from the United States.

One of the Americans was William A. Dudde, a Lutheran missionary on furlough from Argentina, where he had been a pastor, evangelist, and literacy worker for seven years. He obtained his master's from Syracuse, emphasizing religious journalism because at that time the university gave less attention than today to what is called literacy journalism. He worked for Religious News Service in New York as its Protestant news editor and then did public relations work for his denomination in the same city. When Hislop College, an affiliated institution of Nagpur University in Nagpur, India, needed another teacher of journalism for the department of journalism founded there in 1952, Bill Dudde was invited for a two-year term as assistant professor. Hislop, a Christian college, was eager for the department to assist missionaries as well as nationals with communications, including literacy methods and production of materials for new literates. He remained, eventually becoming department head. From there he moved to Geneva, Switzerland, to direct the Lutheran World Federation's news bureau. After that he came back to the United States to work as a Lutheran organization publicist and editor; he has been chief editor of that denomination's magazine, *Resource*.

In later years there came to the Syracuse program students from Uganda, Liberia, Ethiopia, Nigeria, and other sections of Africa; from India, the Philippines, Puerto Rico, Peru, Bolivia, and many other lands. North Americans, in turn, have gone through the program and now do literacy or journalistic work on other continents.

Meanwhile, Robert S. Laubach, son of Dr. and Mrs. Frank C. Laubach, joined the student body. (See the Biographical Background on Robert Laubach in this

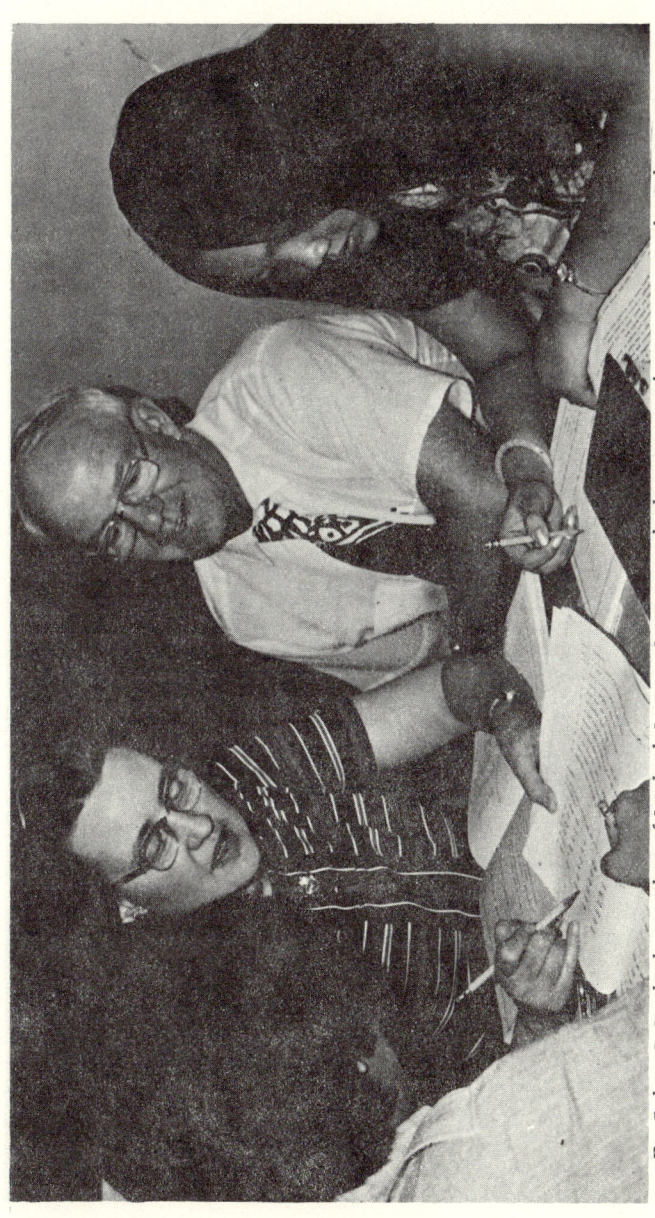

Dr. Robert S. Laubach, president of Laubach Literacy International, observing a volunteer tutor in the Salvation Army teaching center, Pasadena, California. The two students with them are Vietnamese.

BIOGRAPHICAL BACKGROUND

Son of a Famous Father Also Becomes Noted

Children of the famous often have difficulties in life that do not trouble persons not favored with noted parents.

But Robert S. Laubach, son of Frank C. Laubach, known worldwide as a missionary of literacy, has made a place for himself in that sphere. He has reached the point where "Dr. Laubach" might mean himself or his late father, since he has gained wide recognition and is out of the long shadow cast by "Dr. Frank," as he often was called.

Like his father, "Dr. Bob," a shortcut name he has acquired, has as his aim "the eradication of illiteracy throughout the world," as he has phrased his objective.

When Dr. Frank Laubach began his adult literacy program among the Muslims in the Philippines in 1929 he introduced some far-reaching educational innovations. He set persons just become literate to teach their peers. His programs were largely on a volunteer basis; they encouraged students to employ their newly acquired ability to read so as to improve their daily lives. The method became known as "Each One Teach One." So successful was his work then that it was desired elsewhere. Between 1930 and his death in 1970 Dr. Frank Laubach visited and worked in more than one hundred countries, helping develop the Laubach method in more than three hundred languages.

His son recalls that his father's programs were begun by government agencies, by private and mission organizations, and by various labor, social, police, and military groups. "Whatever the sponsoring agency, the programs had in common the dedication to serve illiterates by mobilizing and training literate volunteers to use teaching materials specially prepared for each language group,"

Robert Laubach explains.

The younger Laubach's approach differs from his father's. His emphasis is on "the development of special communication tools for an estimated eight hundred million adults, or two out of five of the world's population." His father emphasized the achievement of literacy all over the world. But it was not possible for the father's efforts to extend to a follow-up program on a wide enough scale. It is here that "Dr. Bob" is making his impact.

His basic training in literacy education was received when he was a boy living in the Philippines, where he was born in Manila in 1918. He accompanied his father on literacy team assignments of the Committee on World Literacy and Christian Literature of the National Council of Churches in Africa and India from 1947 to 1951. These teams helped develop basic primers to be used in teaching adults in many countries. During the tours, the younger Laubach says, he "became convinced of the futility of promising literacy programs where no follow-up, easy-to-read material, trained writers, and publishers of such material existed."

His early schooling began in Manila, was continued at Brent School in Baguio and Lanao High School, Dansalan, also in the Philippines. In 1936 he transferred to Wyoming Seminary at Kingston, Pennsylvania, and then attended Princeton University and the College of Wooster, receiving his BA in 1941. His next two degrees came from Syracuse University: an MA in 1954 from the School of Journalism and a PhD from the School of Education in 1963.

While a Syracuse graduate in 1951 he conceived the idea of a seminar in literacy communications and obtained faculty permission to try out such a course. From that developed two new, fully recognized courses that comprise the core of the present Literacy Communications Program, both of which he still teaches. The twenty-fifth anniversary of the program was reached in the 1976-77 academic year. The materials which developed from his classes and practical work are numerous.

A class project inspired the founding of *News for You* in 1959. It ever since has been the only United States easy-to-read weekly newspaper intended particularly for adults and in 1976 was reaching an average of fifty thousand adult new readers regularly in most states. Similar publications have been patterned after it in a number of nations in South America, Africa, and Asia.

Dr. Robert Laubach, in 1955, helped organize what now is known as Laubach Literacy Incorporated and has become a member of its board. Four years later he organized New Readers Press, the publishing division of LLI. It issues *News for You* as well as much other literature. He is publisher. In 1963 he became executive director of LLI and in 1970, the year of his father's death, he was named president of the board.

Robert Laubach's first important book, titled *Toward World Literacy*, written with his father, was published in 1962. It is a training text. Later he revised and updated *The New Streamlined English Series*, a 15-book effort to simplify English begun by Dr. Frank Laubach. This series is described as "the

chapter). From one of the religious journalism classes he developed "Writing for New Literates," a pioneer course that served as the basis for one taught by Professor Harold Ehrensperger just a few months later at Hislop in India, for he was one of the two American teachers who staffed the original department of journalism at that college.

Among the United States citizens who enrolled at Syracuse for either or both of its special programs in the early days were Doris Hess, Robert Crawford, and Robert Bontrager. Miss Hess and Mr. Crawford, at different times, went to the Philippines, not as much as literacy materials writers and methods teachers as core material used by trained volunteers teaching English. ... It provides a complete reading and writing program, leading the illiterate from zero literacy to the ability to read the newspapers."

He has published numerous short works, including papers issued by UNESCO in Paris, articles for the *Encyclopedia of Education* and the *International Encyclopedia of Higher Education*, and contributed a chapter to the book *Literacy Resources*, issued in 1976 by the International Institute for Literacy Studies in Iran.

Another aspect of his communications work is in public speaking, for he appears on the programs of basic education groups throughout the United States and has taken part in literacy communications conferences, institutes, and workshops in Mexico and Colombia in Latin America; in the African nations of Ghana, Nigeria, Rhodesia, South Africa, Mali, Egypt, Ethiopia, Kenya, and Togo; and the Asian countries of India, Pakistan, and the Philippines.

He sees the work he is attempting to do as part of a "dynamic struggle to provide basic, essential problem-solving tools for the poor majority of the world."

---

straight religious journalists and publicists. Robert Bontrager, who had worked in the Congo, returned to serve in literature work through the years of civil war there, later to come back to Syracuse for his doctorate in communications. He now is an associate professor of journalism at Kansas State University.

When Miss Hess was captured by the idea of becoming a missionary journalist she already had to her credit several years of newspaper work on a small daily and some undergraduate study of journalism. Among the earliest to receive her master's in journalism with the religious emphasis. She was assigned to the Philippines by the United Methodist board, the first person to be so designated by it and so consecrated. Since 1950 she has been guiding workshops for persons who have religious journalism, literature, or literacy responsibilities; preparing literature; advising on religious publications in many nations; and doing other work her training has enabled her to perform. Earlier she had studied religion and missions. In 1964 she completed her doctoral work in communications, also at Syracuse. She now is executive secretary for communications of the World Division of the United Methodist Church Board of Global Ministries. She also heads the Print Media Development Unit of the World Association for Christian Communications.

Bob Crawford and his young wife and baby went to the Philippines in 1954 under the aegis of eight mission boards or organizations to do literature work for them jointly, with headquarters in Manila. From there he was sent by his own denomination, the United Church of Christ, to Indonesia to do similar work. He was what might be called an ecumenical missionary journalist. He, too, later used his furlough time to obtain a PhD degree and became an associate professor of journalism at Cornell University's agricultural college.

Another Pioneering Task

In the early days of journalism, editors and writers were motivated by religious zeal. Journalism, meaning only printed communications then, was a mission for many of them. Later, it became a business; except in the realm of religion itself it has lost most of its missionary zeal as the necessity for economic survival or the desire for greater profits has forced its owners to give first attention to earnings. But in the newer days of missionary

The Missionary Communicatiors 149

journalism and communications there is a chance to recapture the ideals of past years.

Is there an opportunity for service for the idealistic young man or woman of talent in missionary communications? Are there really jobs to be done? Can one earn a living? Would-be communications missionaries deserve honest answers.

Let us put such questions in a proper setting. Not only are numerous Protestant and Catholic missions groups doing literature work on various continents under official denominational auspices, but such activities are carried on as well by other religious bodies.

One of the most effective of the official organizations of the National Council of Churches is Intermedia (long known as the Commission on World Literacy and Christian Literature), with headquarters in New York City. It arranged for a number of American-trained religious and literacy journalists to be sent to other lands to run workshops and lead conferences; guide editors, writers, and artists; help organize literacy programs; and direct literature distribution. Individuals who have been sponsored directly, or, as more often occurs, sent via their own denominations, have become writers for and editors of religious newspapers and periodicals, illustrators of religious materials, and trainers of literature distributors. Intermedia always is interested in knowing about skilled persons who wish to devote their lives to such work.

Another important organization, one of a number of independent groups, is Evangelical Literature Overseas, known commonly as ELO. It sponsors similar activities from its headquarters in Wheaton, Illinois. Founded in 1953, it cooperates with the Interdenominational Missions Association and the Evangelical Missions Association in their literature promotion programs. From time to time ELO announces positions open in the field.

Other indepehdent groups are the Christian Literature Crusade, Sudan Interior Mission, Wycliffe Bible Translators, the Summer Institute of Linguistics, and the David C. Cook Foundation. These, also, attempt to enlist the services of trained communications persons in the United States as well as in the countries served.

Some missionaries with writing gifts return from the field and produce books about their experiences or life in the countries where they served. One such writer is Mrs. Ruth Semands. With her husband, J. T. Semands, Mrs. Semands was a missionary to India. She herself published a book about their experiences, *Missionary Mama,* which was so successful that it led to other books brought out by standard publishers.

Another missionary-writer is Professor Omar Eby, of Eastern Mennonite College, who served for some years in Somalia. While on furlough from that African nation he obtained a master's degree in journalism, using his African experiences and knowledge for some of his fiction and nonfiction in class assignments. So far he has published six books. *A Covenant of Despair* is an adult novel; *How Full the River,* a nonfiction book, describes the life of a foreigner in Africa; *A House in Hue* presents a fictionalized account of the siege in that South Vietnam city; *Sense and Incense* recounts the lives and problems of missionaries; *The Sons of Adam* is a collection of short stories about Americans in Africa; and *Whisper in a Dry Land* tells of a missionary who lost his life to a religious fanatic.

Opportunities Are Real

Opportunities for service do exist. The jobs are real; one can earn a living, but usually it is a spare one. Frequently the service is dependent upon gifts from the church people of the home country. The story told here of the work done by Doris Hess, Bill Dudde, Ruth Eshenaur, and others in the mission field should show that communications talent is needed and will be used. It is needed not merely in the direct way in which they give it. As any missions board secretary will attest, medical, educational, evangelistic, and other missionaries in more conventional areas than communications rarely are equipped to write about their work. Missionaries simply are not necessarily blessed with writing ability. Yet they have much to say, many warming and even frightening experiences, as steady reading of such magazines as *Mission, Maryknoll, New World Outlook, The Missionary Messenger,* and *The Commission,* among others, will show. They need help in telling their stories to the church people at home. They need to know how to create better public relations in their mission areas.

So far, the concept of the missionary communicator has gained comparatively little support from boards of foreign or home missions, although printing, broadcasting, language, and reading unite the world. A few denominations, such as the Seventh-day Adventists, are exceptional in their realization of the world mission of communications media. But most church bodies still fail to appreciate fully the possibilities of missionary communications.

Thus it is that most persons do not think of communications as a mission field. But it always has been this way with pioneers, who would not be pioneers if there had been immediate acceptance and models for what they want to do.

As the Laubachs, Floyd Shacklock, Alfred Moore, Frederick Rex, Marion Van Horne, Harold B. Street, Dennis Clark, Jim Johnson, Robert Walker, and other leaders have realized, the work of the missionary communicator is urgent in the world's present condition. Dr. Wesley Sadler, renowned as a literature-literacy-linguist missionary to Africa, has pointed out that "literature often paves the way for health measures, village improvement, and evangelism."

The Kinds of Work

At least some of the work done by a missionary communicator should be evident from the careers described. He or she writes news, gathers information to be publicized, prepares scripts, or plans programs wherein radio, television, film, and tapes can be used; takes photographs; writes curriculum materials; makes drawings, posters, signs, and sketches; does (or directs) research; teaches communications and literature preparation classes; guides publicity work; advises on public relations problems; supervises the publication of leaflets, brochures, newsletters, newspapers, magazines, and books; speaks at meetings—not all of these all of the time but some of them most of the time and all of them at some time.

Initiative, imagination, and versatility are assets needed by all communicators and particularly by missionaries. Surely they are needed then by a combination of the two. Facilities—typewriters, reference books,

The Missionary Communicatiors 153

telephones, and other conveniences and aids taken for granted in industrially well-developed countries—often are lacking in the mission field. Also sometimes missing is understanding by other persons of why the missionary communicator does what he or she does. An odd character—or so that new missionary seems to the others. He or she is likely to avoid, in speaking and writing, the clichés of religion that make so much religious communications commonplace. These reactions to him or her are to be borne by any pioneer. The missionary communicator makes his own duties and tasks. Few persons can tell him how or what to do, since the skills are so specialized.

As with all missionary enterprise, a first requisite for the Christian missionary communicator is what mission boards generally call "a vital Christian experience," which may be interpreted to mean sincerely living as a Christian should live and with full knowledge of what is meant by so doing. Another requirement is knowledge of the faith he or she represents. Christianity sometimes must be interpreted to non-Christians so a grounding in missions and church history and in the meaning of the faith is important.

Glamour is lacking in the lives of many of these communications missionaries. They often wish they could use more of their skills or use them more often. One of them, Marie Moyer, while working in India for the Mennonites, wrote that they often must face such a situation as this: "Teachers work against such odds as poor cooperation from parents, meager financial assistance from the church, almost no teaching aids. Together we will work toward revitalizing the Sunday school."

One of the most often needed tools is a textbook. Such

communications guides may not even exist in a particular country; they then must be imported and usually are not in the local language. Dr. Eshenaur, for example, in her second year in Kenya had to send letters to United States and other schools of journalism and communications for lists of available texts and then obtain those still in print, a time-consuming and costly procedure.

Communications training and experience—the more varied the better—are essential, although they need not be extensive depending upon the local situation, for, as can be realized, in some parts of the globe only the simplest techniques can be used. If literacy journalism is the goal, study of literacy methods and of the area's culture naturally is imperative. These studies cannot all be obtained fully before departure but should be gained eventually, as more and more do on furlough.

How does one start? By telling a pastor or priest of one's interest and asking advice on where to make preparation. Or by communicating with the mission offices of the denomination and asking how to proceed and also by seeking the counsel of interdenominational bodies interested in channeling promising communicators into this field.

More information about the missionary communicators is to be found in:

BOOKS
Frank C. Laubach, *Thirty Years with the Silent Billion*. Westwood, N.J.: Revell, 1960.

Frank C. and Robert S. Laubach, *Toward World Literacy*. Syracuse, N.Y.: Syracuse University Press, 1959.

Marjorie Medary, *Each One Teach One*. New York: Longmans, Green, 1953.

Bengt K. D. Simonsson, *The Way of the Word*. London: United Society for Christian Literature, 1965.

Ruth Ure, *The Highway of Print*. New York: Friendship Press, 1946.

Marion Van Horn, *Write the Vision*. New York: Committee on World Literacy and Christian Literature, 1963.

ARTICLES

Intermedia, April, 1974. Articles by Marion Van Horne and Ann Pipkin.

ELO Bulletin, January 1967. Articles by W. Harold Fuller, Rene Pache, and Jim Johnson.

NOTE

1. *India Shall Be Literate*, Jubbulpore, India: Mission Press, 1940, p. 116.

8 A Foreign Correspondent- Priest Tells His Story

By James P. Colligan, MM

I would like to be able to say I always wanted to be a foreign correspondent, a noted photojournalist, or even a political cartoonist. The truth is, I always wanted to be a priest. I admired those I knew while growing up in a Roman Catholic family in Pittsburgh, Pennsylvania.

After two years of college there, when the time came

Jim Colligan, a Catholic Foreign Missionary Society (Maryknoll) Priest in Japan since 1955, is a writer and photographer whose work appears in major Catholic periodicals. Here he traces his career with the Maryknoll Mission. He attended Duquesne University, Maryknoll Seminary, and Syracuse University, receiving his BA from the University of the State of New York, master of religious education from Maryknoll, and a master of arts in journalism from Syracuse.

Foreign Correspondent-Priest Tells His Story

for me to make a decision, I chose a foreign mission society, officially titled the Catholic Foreign Mission Society of America, but popularly called Maryknoll. Was it wanderlust? Concern for people? The Spirit guiding my decision? I don't know. All three, I suspect. Seven years later, in 1955, I was ordained a priest. With a bachelor's degree in philosophy and a master's in religious education, I was sent to Japan. (I had hoped for an African assignment.)

Two years of Japanese language study overlapped ten of parish activities. My assignment locations ranged from cultural Kyoto to snowbound Hokkaido mining towns, the latter for a period of 3½ years alone. Besides the usual priestly duties, I periodically taught English and English literature in high schools and colleges, was government-approved principal of my parish kindergarten, and an avid observer of Japan and the Japanese.

In the meantime, I developed a conviction that I could match or improve upon the materials on Japan being published in our mission society's magazine, a 50-year-old, widely circulated monthly originally called *The Field Afar*, and later *Maryknoll*. I bought a Rolleiflex and attempted a photo story, scourging myself with a resolve to earn the cost of the camera by getting the results published. It worked. I began using my weekly free day to visit other Hokkaido parishes and civic functions to take photos and do interviews. *Maryknoll* published enough of them during a five-year period that my Japan superior one day asked if I would like to study journalism in the United States.

I said yes immediately, on one condition. I wanted assurance that I would return to Japan, not be given a staff job Stateside. Top authority said okay. Syracuse University's journalism school accepted my application in the fall of 1966. Almost 38 years old and, frankly, a frightened stranger to the United States and its college scene (reverse cultural shock), I went back to school, working weekends at a nearby parish church. I've never been under more work pressure than during those months. All deadlines. But good teachers.

Three semesters later I squeaked through the degree requirements and returned to Japan. Superiors had changed in the meantime. My new boss said, "Jim, I don't know what you're going to do here with that degree." I wasn't sure myself, but I was not going to tell anyone else that. I spent a few days drawing up a job description which, eight years later, still has validity. He bought it. I took up residence in Tokyo as a self-styled foreign correspondent for the Stateside Catholic press. When NC News (National Catholic News Service) wanted coverage of the Christian Pavilion at Expo '70 in Osaka, I was obliged to make my status official by obtaining Japanese Government accreditation if I wanted Expo accreditation. I have had accreditation since, though not always with NC News. I covered the first papal visit to Manila and Sydney, of Pope Paul VI, scraping up the travel money by promising words or pictures to three different organizations. They got their money's worth; I got tired.

What do I do as a correspondent? Well, from the beginning I've considered myself to be in a publish-or-perish situation. My bosses cooperated by relieving me of parish duties. It was up to me to prove the job was viable. My food and lodging were guaranteed, but I had no budget in the early years and no money of my own. Every postage stamp, every frame of film exposed was painfully used. The utter lack of professionalism that I soon detected in certain areas of the church press was depressing. Finally, the job took from me the human consolation I had experienced as a pastor of souls and spiritual counselor.

I did news articles and news photos, feature articles, and photo essays, and continually tried to find new markets. More than once I cast envious eyes at good-paying secular journals, even applied for, and was called for an interview for, an editor's job with one of Tokyo's four English-language dailies. I decided it would be a cop-out, even journalistically, for I would then be doing what some secular organization wanted me to be doing and not what I thought needed to be done. I know now, with confidence, I could have handled the job.

I spent a frustrating year with the Japan Catholic Bishops' (all Japanese) Conference in its initial attempt to organize a public information office. It was not ready for that yet. The operation collapsed due to differences of opinion among the bishops, especially on editorial authority of the nation's Catholic newspaper. I decided the problem was theirs to solve, chalked up the year to experience, and went back to free-lancing.

I co-edited the *Japan Christian Yearbook* of 1969-70, a combined Catholic-Protestant effort. Rising printing costs and fewer missioners to buy the book made that issue the final one, as far as I know.

If space allowed I would enjoy reviewing some of my more exasperating experiences with church press personnel and publications. Needing to work with them from a distance, I have sets of correspondence as case study documentation. (Someday I may publish a book of them!)

Yet, I have managed to publish photos and articles in newspapers and periodicals willing to pay for them, in the United States, Japan, Germany, and Australia, with some regularity. I confess they have been Catholic publications almost exclusively, not through prejudice, but because I know the Catholic market best and how to deal with it (if anybody does!). Time limitations more than anything else dictated my decisions. Lillian R. Block of Religious News Service (RNS) has been especially kind to remember me with a press card annually, but the only thing I've sent to her organization to date is good intentions, a lapse for which I'm sorry.

In 1972 I informed NC News that we were parting unless better remuneration was offered me. We parted. My only regret is that the English-speaking Catholic press still has no paid professional correspondent in Asia.

Since then, *Maryknoll* has been my primary market for reasons too numerous to recount. Between 1968 and 1975 I have had fifty articles and 350 photos published in it. Over the years we've had differences of opinion on matters like photo credits, reprint rights to photos and articles, and cooperation generally. But overall, *Maryknoll* publishers and editors have functioned as professionals, in my judgment. They have handled my materials with care, replied promptly to queries, given me reasonable payment, even accepted criticism and corrected inequities in some instances. Moreover, with a circulation of a million-plus through membership-type subscriptions, the publication offers its contributors a respected and respectable platform. Of course, my relationship with the staff is more than the ordinary free-lance relationship, so my dealings are in a special category. Nevertheless, the Catholic Church in the United States is well represented by *Maryknoll* in journalism matters, especially pertaining to overseas problems.

I have had free-lance materials published in *Sign, Catholic Digest, World Parish, Our Sunday Visitor* (magazine section), and *The Word in the World* (an annual) in the United States; in *Kontinente, Mission Aktuell, Franziskaner Missionen, Alle Welt,* and *Maria Von Guten Rat* (an annual) in Germany (some of these through an agency called *foto-present);* in *Annals* in Australia; and in *Catholic Graph, Roba no Mimi, Seibo no Kishi, PHP* (secular), and in the newspapers of the Catholic Church and of the Foreign Correspondents' Club in Japan. Photos have played an important part in most of these.

In some instances, articles I've personally liked best sold best. A color photo essay of a Holy Week festival in the Philippines with maybe one hundred words of text has been used three times in the United States and twice in Germany, as of Easter 1976. An article on Shinto with ten good black-and-white photos was rejected by a national Catholic newspaper in the United States but accepted promptly by a Catholic monthly which played it prominently. It later sold in Germany also. (Incidentally, one of the key photos was of the Emperor and Empress of Japan, not an easy photo to get. But three years earlier I attempted and failed to place an article with a top-paying United States secular magazine. The photo was taken on that occasion. I now have close to 1,000 contact sheets and a few thousand good slides.) An article on a Buddhist nun and a Catholic nun has sold four times.

On the other hand, an article on two orphaned, mixed-blood boys in their early teens in Korea sold only to *Maryknoll*. Sons of Korean mothers and American GI's, one white, one black, the two boys are close friends. The story, published in *Maryknoll*, brought queries from American readers. Within a year both boys were adopted, *by the same family*. If it's never used again, I don't care. I did some of the earlier articles too on land reform and social injustice in the Philippines.

My travels have been geared primarily to nations in Asia where Maryknoll personnel are stationed—Japan, Korea, Taiwan, Hong Kong, and the Philippines. I've also managed working trips to Guam, Sri Lanka, Burma, Australia, and Papua-New Guinea (the latter prior to their joint independence). I met President Chiang Kai-shek in Taipei, President Ferdinand Marcos and Pope Paul VI in Manila, and President Gerald Ford in Tokyo. No less important, I've met, interviewed, or photographed hundreds of people of equal worth ultimately, however unknown. And I've met and associated with many fine ladies and gentlemen of the press.

Since mid-1969, my first year with Japanese Government accreditation as a correspondent, I have belonged to the Foreign Correspondents' Club of Japan (FCCJ). I've worked on several club committees, including the committees which revised the Articles of Association and the Bylaws a few years back. Most recently I am chairman of the Foreign Press in Japan (FPIJ), a subsidiary organization which coordinates news-gathering activities outside the FCCJ premises. These include, for example, allocation conferences with Foreign Office officials prior to the state visit of foreign dignitaries (at which the number of reporters and cameramen at a given function are determined), followed then by an allocation meeting of interested correspondents; liaison between the foreign press and government bureaus for periodic briefings; liaison with the Japanese press club, and so on.

My official designation is foreign correspondent for Maryknoll International News Service. My designated responsibilities are simply put: I'm free to decide what stories or photos I care to attempt for whatever publication or organization, so long as I can justify it if asked (I haven't been) and come up with the needed funds. That's a lot of freedom.

Now, I must qualify somewhat. I am still a priest, so I offer Mass daily, albeit privately, unless travel prevents it. I help my boss, for example, my religious superior in Japan, on a fairly regular basis in editing jobs: the Japan Regional News, regional plans, and the like. I am asked occasionally by Japanese individuals to explain Christian doctrine to them on a more-or-less regular basis, a privilege I could not refuse. I attend meetings of Maryknoll personnel in Tokyo at least monthly. Currently I am also responsible for data gathering for a history of Maryknoll in Japan since 1933. Finally, membership in Maryknoll imposes certain "family" obligations which require my presence from time to time. I am also an associate member of the Catholic Press Association of the United States.

Am I faced with any contradictions in my hyphenated situation as priest-journalist? For example, does being a member of a missionary organization oblige me to write only favorable pieces about Catholic Christianity and condemn all other faiths? Am I inevitably in a pulpit when I sit at my typewriter? Does religious journalism mean pietistic advocacy journalism? Are crime and the seedy side of human society outside my sphere because they are not uplifting? Definitely not!

Christians have no monopoly on basic human goodness even if they have a bigger share of divine truth. With my education in philosophy I dare say I have as good a chance of separating fact from opinion as most other reporters have, and a better chance of publishing both than correspondents from communist countries, for example. Nevertheless, journalists affiliated with religious organizations are often classified as goody-goodies, inveterate idealists, or goodwilled amateurs in press circles. Often the classification is deserved, as much by the insipid publication as by the ingenuous individual. I do not believe in hiding my religious affiliation but I do not flaunt it either. That's not a compromise. Nor does it deny a place to religious propaganda in the vast scheme of journalistic endeavors. But advertising and reporting are usually distinguishable, even when the advertising is perfectly truthful. Justifiably or not, reporters tend to disdain "PR types." The religious journalist then should be very clear in his or her own mind which one he or she is doing on any given project. The advantage of being Christian, as I see it, is this: if what we believe is really true, then truth can only help us, not hurt us, in the long haul. Commercial advertising so permeates the ubiquitous media today that even unsophisticates smell propaganda promptly and tend to suspect it. I believe reliable reporting geared to the listener and viewer can be as effective today among educated people as outright propaganda intends.

What successes can I count since 1968? Not many, other than materials published *for pay*. Why, I've been asked, do you insist on payment when you're a priest with a roof over your head, no family to feed, and supposedly dedicated to sharing your insights, observations, reflections? In reply, I give two reasons, both based on experience. First, good cameras, good film, and good processing cost money. Postage from Japan is high. I have yet to meet the camera store owner or postal official who refuses to bill me because of my Christian vocation. Nor should they refuse. Moreover, I cannot take photos of a child welfare center in northern Japan or interview a rural minister in Kyushu while sitting at home in Tokyo. Round-trip fare today might cost $120. How much more for foreign travel! As a priest I have the advantage of being welcome in the rectories of most priests around the world, so I avoid major hotel bills. Furthermore, they provide grassroots contacts. Should I be allowed to impose upon their generosity for a few days or a few weeks for free because I'm doing stories? Not at all.

My second reason reinforces that first. Publications do not respect materials they receive for free. Like passing out handbills on the street, there's little hope of estimating their worth. Put another way, giveaways are considered PR materials, propaganda. Somewhere along the way, too many members of the U.S. Catholic press have come to view the missions and missioners as poor relations, somewhat like the underdeveloped countries to which many missioners are sent. I have had editors of U.S. Catholic papers say to me, "You want materials on

Japan published? Send them along." "What are your rates?" I've asked. "Sorry, that's your responsibility," they've replied. Even if I could afford to give them away, I would not, as a rule.

I am sympathetic to the financial burden some editors carry, but the responsibility to inspire missionary ideals, foreign and domestic, in readers is that of the editor. Mission is a fundamental Christian concept, not a PR project. Individual diocesan papers may have trouble financing foreign coverage on a regular basis, but the news services and national papers had better find a way. They are still paying a pittance on a stringer basis, settling for amateurish releases passing as news. No wonder their subscribers' papers don't sell. Meantime, across the world church leaders are touting the importance of communications like paperboys peddling extras.

As a correspondent, I would like to stand alongside the *New York Times*, *U.S. News and World Report*, AP and UPI bureau chiefs, all acquaintances here in Tokyo, and say, "I'm with the U.S. Catholic press," or "I'm with the religious press of the United States," and know that my interviewee is equally eager that *my* publications carry his views. More likely at present, his response would be, "You're with what?!" The bishops and faithful of the English-speaking Christian world can complain about the treatment of church matters in the media, can worry that the truth is not being told due to the influence of big business on the press. But until they have a topflight press of their own, their cries are a voice in the wilderness.

Well, that's the darker side. The bright side is, I have not yet had to compromise principles, either of faith or of

Father James P. Colligan, MM, interviewing Tomejiro Kobayashi, a Japanese coal miner. They are in Mr. Kobayashi's home in Yubari, a city on the island of Hokkaido; left to right, Mrs. Kobayashi, Isumi (their daughter), Mr. Kobayashi, Father Colligan, an unidentified miners union representative, and Father Gudalefsky (a local Catholic priest).

professionalism. I'm writing, photographing, and having my materials published. Not the latest "hot" facts necessarily, until we utilize our potential for a worldwide news organization, but truth and basic truths, hopefully in a new guise or from a fresh angle. Hopefully too with some depth. Occasionally, even at this distance from my readers, I learn that my views are being read. I am not starving to death just yet. What more could a foreign correspondent-priest ask?

9 Free-Lance Writers About Religion

Every would-be writer should have on a wall of his room a large sign that reads:

> You Can't Make
> A Living as a
> Free-Lance Writer
> About Religion

The free lance is an unattached writer, paid piecemeal for what he composes, and is not on salary with any one publication. Some writers do free-lance work in addition to their regular occupation, but they are not then full-time free-lancers.

Free-lancing, whether it be about religion or any other topic, if it is one's only source of income is a hazardous occupation in even the best of times. Few writers, either secular or religious, can depend upon it to pay all their bills. So far as the author has been able to learn, no one ever has made a successful career, financially speaking, of free-lance writing solely about religion or the church. Scores of writers have sustained themselves well through free-lancing and have written religious articles or stories, but about half their copy had to do with other topics. Every free lance on religion known to the author depends for the bulk of his income upon a regular post as a clergyman, teacher, administrator, or some secular journalistic connection.

Free-lance writing about religion is so risky, in fact, that no one should give up a regular income for it. To do so would be almost certain economic suicide. But it is a pleasant sideline for earning small checks most of the time and bringing in a big one occasionally. Obviously far more important, it is a way to influence readers, listeners, or viewers not otherwise reachable with one's ideas. And it is fun as well as work, for it is creative as well as upsetting to the nerves and hard on one's patience.

Why are free-lance articles about religion so ill-paid except for the occasional writer? Chiefly because most religious publications are small, have comparatively low budgets for copy, earn only modest revenue from circulation and advertising, face steadily rising costs for materials, and, in some instances, are managed by administrators unaware or indifferent to the merit of paying writers adequately. Printers and the postal service set their own rates and go to law if they are not paid; writers not on salary must accept the rates of the publisher unless they can get a better rate elsewhere, which has only limited possibilities. Few writers belong to organizations formed in behalf of writers who free-lance, and such organizations have contracts only with the largest firms and not the nonprofit press such as that of religion or education.

In the next chapter are facts and figures about the rates paid for certain kinds of materials. Whether the publications could pay more is not the issue at this point, however. The fact is that they do not, although payments are better than they ever have been, even if not good enough in days of inflation.

The rewards come not in the checks so much as in the minds reached, the friends made, the pleasure or instruction or inspiration given, the influence exerted. Such returns will be unimpressive to persons who do—or are forced to do—nothing unless it brings cash in quickly. But to people who need not depend heavily upon free-lancing, the intangible returns are far more valuable and exciting than any amount of money.

The sort of life the religious free-lancer leads can be judged from the careers of a few writers who have been at it for some years.

Garrison and Everett

Webb Garrison—known to some readers through a pseudonym, Gary Webster—told the publishers of *Contemporary Authors* that he would "rather sit at a typewriter than play golf or watch a football game." The writing that gives him the greatest satisfaction, he has said, is on "scientific topics treated with accuracy, but interpreted from a theistic point of view showing that there is no conflict between good science and good religion."

Dr. Garrison served as a Methodist pastor in South Carolina for four years before becoming assistant dean of the Candler School of Theology at Emory University. Five years later he joined the staff of the board of education of his denomination, then was named president of McKendree College. In three more years he returned to the pastorate and more intensive writing, although during much of this time he was a columnist for newspapers and magazines and producing books, some under the Gary Webster cognomen. These volumes have been on various aspects of religion or language, such as *What's in a Word*. His articles have appeared in national consumer and specialized, mainly religious, periodicals.

Glenn D. Everett is the type of free lance who does not rely, as do most others, on a full-time professional position. He is a free lance in different activities. Early in his career he was a secular as well as a religious communicator. He found his way into journalism because of a perceptive, creative editor, the late David D. Baker. Dr. Baker, editor of *The Messenger* (later incorporated into the *United Church Herald*), was the type of editorial executive who helped develop young writers by publishing their work. While Mr. Everett was an undergraduate at Heidelberg College, Dr. Baker reprinted an article Glenn had written for the college paper and encouraged him to contribute others. It was then that his free-lancing began.

By the end of the next decade this writing developed such volume that he could open his own office in Washington. But during that decade he worked hard. He accumulated practical experience as a correspondent for the Brainerd, Minnesota, *Daily Dispatch;* St. Louis *Globe-*

Democrat; Des Moines *Register;* and for two magazines before their merger, *United States News* and *World Report*. He also was an assistant to Bascom Timmons, a veteran Washington correspondent. This work included foreign correspondence in what now are considered behind-the-iron-curtain nations.

He moved into religious communications by becoming the Washington correspondent for Religious News Service and was its only full-time staffer outside the headquarters offices in New York. He also began contributing free-lance articles to *Look, Saturday Evening Post, The Christian Century,* and other magazines to supplement his RNS income. He also was Washington correspondent for a string of secular dailies published in small cities.

Not satisfied—and also needing all this work, being a man with a family living in an expensive city, the national capital—Mr. Everett for some years also provided about fifteen church publications with a syndicated column, "Religion in Stamps," helped produce films, ran a postcard and Christmas card publishing firm which later burgeoned into a substantial business and wrote books.

Glenn Everett is one of the religious free-lancers who has not studied journalism or religion, but much of his copy has appeared in the religious press or about religion in the secular publications. Nor has he served in the ministry. An Ohioan born in 1921, he went to the University of Iowa after finishing his undergraduate work at Heidelberg in his native state, and obtained a master's in political science. He learned journalistic techniques while at work (*i.e.,* the hard way) and was able to hold positions of various sorts on different types of publications. Thus he had a varied background to bring to free-lancing. He has had to curtail some of his work in recent years because of an unusual eye difficulty which handicaps his reading.

The McDermott Career

A man who became one of the nation's foremost freelance writers on religion for magazines flunked his first year of college English. This fact may encourage readers who have had similar troubles.

A well-meaning English teacher told the freshman in the solemn, sage manner some professors use: "Be sure that whatever else you do, you never try to write for a living, Bill."

But he went on to become a daily newspaper reporter in Chicago and then to earn his living as a contributor to some of the world's largest magazines, such as *Reader's Digest, Good Housekeeping, McCall's,* and several dozen others just as prominent. He was one of the few financially successful free-lancers of his time.

Bill was clergyman William F. McDermott, of Oak Park, Illinois. He is quoted elsewhere in this book. Once he told an interviewer that "in the varied fields of the Christian ministry, nothing gives greater satisfaction than the ministry of the printed word."

A quick look at his career will show what a combination of writing ability, journalistic imagination and inquisitiveness, and human experience can do. McDermott was born in Winfield, Kansas, before the turn of the century. All the men in his family had been lawyers; none was either a minister or a communicator. After reporting news for papers in Winfield and Kansas City, he enrolled at McCormick Seminary, Chicago, and served his first church in the city's stockyards area.

But the journalist in him would not down. So, like Irwin St. John Tucker, the Episcopal priest who worked for years as a copyeditor on Chicago papers, Mr. McDermott held two full-time jobs: as reporter for the Chicago *Daily News* and as minister and guest preacher in Bohemian and Italian mission churches and in Presbyterian ones as well.

After World War I he returned to the *Daily News*, then did missions publicity for the United Methodist Church, and followed that by rejoining the paper as religious news editor in 1928. He remained until 1945 and became known nationally for his religious writing. He had been free-lancing on the side with increasing success, so in 1945 he broke away from staff work to engage in full-time free-lancing for magazines. In his time he published more than five hundred major magazine articles on religious, scientific, welfare, and educational subjects. Many of these pieces were personality sketches for both the secular and religious press. But note that he had to split his outlets between them.

"Stories are everywhere," he wrote the author of this book. "I found a good *Reader's Digest* story in a 2-inch item in a New York paper about the dedication of a chapel outside Clinton Prison (Dannemora, N.Y.). *Digest* ran my story, 'Church of the Good Thief' . . ." he related.

Persistence, without which free-lancers surely fail, is illustrated by his experience in trying to place that article. The *Digest* was not interested in the idea when approached. Another magazine asked to see it, but rejected it. He then sent the typescript to the *Digest,* which on seeing it in final form liked it and paid him $1,200 for it.

Now and then a writer about religious subjects who may not be an eminent theologian or clergyman-educator or head of a church body gains a measure of prominence through his work. One such was Hartzell Spence, whose book, *One Foot in Heaven,* was a best seller. It was the first of several by Spence (he also wrote *Story of America's Religion* and *The Clergy and What They Do).* Mr. Spence's background was unlike those of the other writers in this chapter. A Phi Beta Kappa graduate of the University of Iowa, he worked for United Press International for eleven years. He was founder and editor of the army newspaper, *Yank.* His articles appeared in numerous major magazines, both secular and religious.

A Teacher and a Free-Lancer

To combine teaching and free-lancing generally is difficult, although this may depend upon whether the teacher works in primary, secondary, or higher education. By the time an educator is enough of an expert in his specialty to free-lance he may be so busy with administrative and other nonteaching duties he has no time for the typewriter. Some resourceful educators continue to write, even if not full time. One such was the late Robert W. Root.

An Iowan, he wrote his first novel at nine; at least he thought that was what it was. The taste of this amateurish effort moved him to decide that journalism was his field. And so it was. He chose newspaper work.

BIOGRAPHICAL BACKGROUND

Free-Lance Reviewer of Religious Books

People who do not make their livings as professional writers but have writing skills and an interest or occupation that is useful to a writer can contribute to society nevertheless. The obvious examples are the pastor who writes on the side for either secular or religious publications or some other medium and the religious education or church school officer who contributes to the journals of that occupation. But there are other possibilities.

A church librarian can prepare reviews of religious books. The returns may be only pin money or copies of new books sent for review by publishers, but the service it offers is valuable to readers of new volumes. Lay persons, using new library books from outside the church collection, can do the same. Some contribute such reviews to their parish papers or magazines or a statewide denominational publication. Others write for the secular press.

Mrs. Connie Soth, a native Oregonian now living in Bea-

Not until he had been in it a number of years did he turn to a career in religious communications.

More or less accidentally, he related, he did church reporting when, after his first degree at Iowa State in 1936, he enrolled at Columbia University's Graduate School of Journalism. Noting that each Monday's New York *Times* carried coverage of sermons preached the day before, he applied for a part-time reporting job. For the rest of the college year, directed by the *Times* city desk, he trekked around Manhattan from church to church Sunday mornings for $5 a story.

verton but originally of Portland, has shown how that can be done by a free-lancer. She was inspired by the work of Dr. Frank C. Laubach, the noted missionary who battled illiteracy all over the world (see chapter 7). She took a writing course in the hope of calling more attention to his work. She decided, however, that a full-blown career as an author was not within her reach. Instead she began placing articles about Dr. Laubach's work with her local paper, *The Valley Times*, a widely circulated weekly.

Meanwhile, she had been serving as librarian of an American Lutheran Church in Beaverton, St. Matthew, since 1962. It is an activity closely related to her writing and one which interests her deeply. It has brought her opportunities to teach in workshops of church librarian organizations.

One day she approached Mrs. Lida Belle Swain, women's and church pages editor

---

When he completed his master's degree in 1937 he received along with it a Pulitzer scholarship, which paid for a year in Europe. His first full-time journalism job was as a reporter for the Des Moines *Tribune*. On the side he directed youth activities in a local church. From that came a front-page series about a young people's crusade against pinball machines.

During the early years of World War II he served as city hall reporter, but became restless to do something more significantly related to the world crisis. By 1943 he had become an editorial writer for both the *Register* and *Tribune* in Des Moines. He still hoped to go into overseas relief work; finally he was offered a public relations post with the Department of Reconstruction and Inter-Church Aid of the World Council of Churches. Soon after the war ended he arrived with the first group of

for *The Valley Times*, and with some hesitation proposed a column devoted to reviews of books which as she now puts it, "would tell readers about good, wholesome books ... a welcome relief from all the literary garbage glutting the market. ..." Mrs. Swain was receptive, asked for trial reviews, and in 1971 Mrs. Soth's first column appeared, entitled "Bookworm's Buffet."

The column has been running under that title ever since and is paid for at space rates. It is one of many activities for Mrs. Soth's church and family. She is the wife of Forrest Soth, assistant office supervisor for Texaco at its Portland marketing terminal, and the mother of three grown sons.

"My policy," she explains, "is to review only those books which I consider will build faith, show how Christ's love reaches us through other people, and restores hope to the hopeless."

American staffers sent to Geneva, Switzerland.

Bob traveled for the World Council to the various war-ravaged sections, took hundreds of photographs, and wrote countless news stories and articles aimed at stimulating American church giving. To broaden coverage, he developed an informal syndicate of up to eighteen United States church magazines for ecumenical stories and pictures and served as Geneva correspondent for *The Christian Century*.

When his two-year stint was over, he set out for a free-lance year in the Near East and Asia. Serving as special correspondent for *The Christian Science Monitor*, he also provided features and pictures for the International Committee of the YMCA, the religion desk of *Newsweek*, and various Protestant magazines and mission boards.

On his return to the United States he became executive editor of Worldover Press, a syndicate providing constructive news to many church publications. This nonprofit organization, headed by a veteran religious and international journalist, Devere Allen, sought to set an example in the syndicate and news agency field as the *Monitor* does in the newspaper world. Bob continued to free-lance at the same time.

The turn into teaching came in 1952. He joined the Syracuse University journalism faculty as an associate professor in the magazine department. He later became head of its religious journalism program, all the time doing article and critical writing as well as producing books. Among the results was *How to Make Friends Abroad,* which drew upon his work as a religious news reporter overseas.

This prolific writer published many more articles and reviews, and several more books, until his death in 1966. The books included *Progress Against Prejudice* and *Struggle of Decency,* both dealing with the church and race, and texts on magazine and newspaper editing. He wrote reviews for *Saturday Review, The Christian Century,* and other publications, and contributed professional articles frequently to professional journals in communications. At the university he began a new program, one related to both journalism and religion, which prepared people for mental health information work, and conducted occasional religious journalism conferences and meetings, such as summer short courses for religious editors and publishers. He also obtained his PhD and a full professorship. In his final years he left Syracuse to teach at Eisenhower College.

Clergymen's Wives and Other Free-Lancers

The clergyman's wife is in a better position than many women to write free-lance material about religion. And for that reason she often is among the regular contributors to religious publications and the author of books for children and youth. Obtaining first-hand experience and ideas, even access to a specialized library, is easy for her.

Mrs. Margaret Anderson, wife of an Evangelical Covenant pastor in California, is a prolific writer who is an example. Author of an invaluable book for religious writers, *The Christian Writer's Handbook*, she has drawn on her long experience. She has contributed articles and stories to scores of denominational periodicals for both adults and children, and is author of other books, including *Bill and Betty Learn About God*, *It's Your Business*, *Teen-ager Bill*, and others in paperback.

A Southern Baptist author who has taken advantage of her place as a pastor's wife is Mrs. Ollin D. Owens, who under the name Loulie Latimer Owens made two characters, "the Rev. Percy Vere" and his wife, "Minnie Belle," familiar to thousands in that denomination. These humorous sketches appeared in the official monthly, *The Baptist Program*, and also were gathered to become a book, *Minnie Belle*. In recent years she has turned to more serious subjects, particularly church history. She wrote most of the November 1975 issue of the *Journal* of the South Carolina Baptist History Society; in 1971 the South Carolina Baptist Convention published her book, *Saints of Clay: The Shaping of South Carolina Baptists*. She has contributed to *Home Life* and other religious periodicals as well.

Another effective Southern Baptist free-lance is Mrs.

BIOGRAPHICAL BACKGROUND

Free-Lance Columnist, Article Writer, Photographer

Most journalists, whether beginners or veterans, have a secret desire. It is to have their own column. Writers on religion are no exception, but few achieve that goal.

In this chapter are details about a few writers who have become columnists with national distribution of their work, such as Louis Cassels of United Press International. Most such columns offer sermonettes, like the work of Billy Graham and Elisha P. Douglass.

But less widely known is another handful of writers whose work is seen only regionally, yet is of value and influence. One of these is Isabel Champ, who regularly writes a general column as well as a religion column, in addition to articles now and then for the religion press.

Mrs. Champ's "Gospel Truth" appears weekly in the Portland *Oregon Journal,* a large northwestern United States daily. Her secular column is seen in the Salem (Ore.) *Statesman* and in the Canby (Ore.) *Herald.* Her articles have been published in *Decision, Christian Life, Guideposts, Farm Journal,* and other periodicals.

She came to religion writing from a background of radio and television work in Kansas and Oregon, where she was a camera operator, wrote commercials, and had her own programs. One day in 1972 she decided to enroll in a creative writing class offered evenings at a community college near her home in Mulino, Oregon. In that course she wrote her first article. At the suggestion of

Marjorie Moore Armstrong. As Marjorie Moore she was assistant editor of *Baptist Student* and then managing editor of *The Commission,* the international magazine of

her teacher, the late Florence K. Palmer, she sent it to *Decision* and it was accepted. Let Mrs. Champ relate the rest:

"... a couple of months after this, *Guideposts* announced its national writing contest. My teacher encouraged me to enter. I did and won. It was a full-expense paid trip to New York and a week's study with such writers as Catherine Marshall, Arthur Gordon, Leonard LeSourd, Jamie Buckingham, and John and Elizabeth Sherrill. ... Twenty of us throughout North America won this trip. ... Mrs. Sherrill was assigned as my personal teacher."

Before she left the exciting week of training, she heard Mr. Buckingham say, "A weekly newspaper column is excellent writing discipline." So when she went home Mrs. Champ offered to be a columnist for the local newspaper, *The Canby Herald*. The editor was delighted. As a result, "In Champ's Corner" has been running ever since in the paper. Her columns later won an Oregon newspaper contest, the best local column award.

"Gospel Truth," her religion column, appeared first in the Portland *Oregon Journal*. She continued to write articles and now is able to say, as few free-lancers can, "Whenever I submit an article to a magazine, it usually sells on its first or second time out."

Isabel Champ believes that God has given her the ability to write. "That's one reason I write," she says, and adds, "Another reason is that I simply like to write."

A graduate of McPherson College in Kansas, she has had no journalistic training aside from that one creative writing class. She not only writes but also takes photographs that illustrate some of her writings; these too have brought her honors.

Her husband, John G. Champ, Sr., is a carpenter by

the Board of Foreign Missions. Earlier she had earned a master's degree at the Medill School of Journalism of Northwestern University. During those years and since

occupation and an active churchman who, like her, belongs to the Christian & Missionary Alliance Church in nearby Canby. They have two sons. Kelly lives with his own family near Mulino and John, Jr., a helicopter pilot connected with the Wycliff Bible Translators, in 1976 went to Papua—New Guinea, taking his wife and two little daughters.

Isabel Champ's writing is friendly in tone, filled with human interest, and at times witty without being silly or sarcastic. She selects everyday experiences, but avoids excessive preachiness. Her subjects grow out of her family life, her church work, and her associations in her community.

---

she has contributed articles to various periodicals and newspapers, both religious and secular. Her latest book, published in 1976, is *School Someday*, written for her denomination's Foreign Missions Graded Series. She lives in a journalistic atmosphere, for her husband is O. K. Armstrong, long an article writer for *Reader's Digest* and other magazines and an author of several books, one in collaboration with his wife, *Baptists Who Shaped a Nation*.

Two other pastors' wives who have published books are Mary Jean Irion and Dorothy Clarke Wilson. Mrs. Irion, author of *From the Ashes of Christianity* and *Yes, World, a Mosaic of Meditation*, also is known as a poet. She contributes to *The Christian Century* and other magazines of religion and has appeared in *Ladies' Home Journal, Literary Review*, and other secular magazines. Mrs. Wilson is a widely successful biographer. Her better known books include *Dr. Ida: The Story of Dr. Ida Scudder; Lone Woman: The Story of Elizabeth Blackwell; Palace of Healing: The Story of Dr. Clara Swain; Take*

My Hands: Dr. Mary Verghese; Bright Eyes: The Story of Susette L'Flesche; and *Handicap Race: The Inspiring Story of Roger Arnett.* She also is a biblical novelist.

For many years Elizabeth Yates—novelist, biographer, and author of other types of books—was a leading member of the faculties of Green Lake and St. David's conferences for religious authors and journalists, as well as of secular meetings of that sort. Miss Yates, whose husband, William McGreal, also wrote books, has had a distinguished literary career to which she adds a volume every year or so. Primarily a book writer, she comes from a literary rather than a communications background, although occasionally she contributes articles to periodicals. Many of her novels and nonfiction books for children as well as adults are aimed at the secular reader and are not obviously religious in content. But they are overlaid with inescapable religious idealism. Among her distinctly religious books are *Your Prayers and Mine,* an anthology she edited; a biography of Howard Thurman, dean of Boston University chapel for many years; and *A Book of Hours,* a volume of devotions published in 1976. Among her widely read earlier books are *The Lighted Heart* and *Amos Fortune, Free Man.* The latter brought her the Newbery Medal as "the most distinguished contribution to American literature for children" in 1951 and now considered a classic of children's literature. It exhibited an understanding of the problems of Afro-Americans years before social changes began to occur in the status of the minority. It also brought her the William Allen White and New York *Herald Tribune* awards.

A native of Buffalo, New York, she has lived much of her life on an old farm in Peterborough, New Hampshire. For a decade she and Mr. McGreal, an American businessman, lived in London and traveled on the continent. Some of her books are placed in her immediate surroundings; she is a painstaking researcher to give her novels as well as her biographies authenticity. She is a member of the Society of Friends.

An example of persistence in a free-lance writer is Mrs. La Vernae Dick, an Oregonian Mennonite who, despite heavy home duties, writes not only for her own denomination's publications but other church publications as well. Along with her writing she has continued her education and training. She attends as well as teaches at

---

BIOGRAPHICAL BACKGROUND

A Religious Communicator Who Uses Most Media

In the days when mass communications demanded talent only with the printed word, careers for the persons of religious conviction were more limited than they are today. The more varied are one's skills the greater the opportunities. To balance that, however, may be the economic situation at any one time and the increasing tendency of employers, both secular and religious, to expect greater versatility and depth and breadth of training.

In Lancaster, Pennsylvania, is a young Mennonite communicator, Merle Good, who may have realized this trend some years ago. As a result, by the late 1970s, he has become a scriptwriter for television and radio, has written nine plays so far, one of them a musical, has written a novel which was made into a motion picture as well, and has produced numerous magazine and newspaper articles. Nor is that all. He also is producer of an annual Dutch

religious writer's conferences and other professional communication and church meetings. Mrs. Dick has specialized in historical and interpretative writing, mainly for use in Christian education.

An Untapped Source

Because they are untrained and inexperienced, a large number of potential free-lance religious communicators are not being used by the world of church communication. They are lost among the millions of retired men and women, of women whose children have reached maturity, and of widows with the leisure to write. Within

---

Family Festival and is associate editor of *Festival Quarterly* magazine. All this work has a religious setting, usually Mennonite, and expresses the particular views of that denomination.

But he has not confined himself to the relatively limited Mennonite communications world. The Washington *Post* in 1976 carried an article, "A Conscientious Objector's View of the Bicentennial," in which he discussed the impact of the national celebration on Mennonite principles. Two years earlier he contributed an essay to another leading United States daily, *The New York Times*, titled "Exploitation and Storytelling." He condemned the exploitation of his people by outsiders who cater to tourists. A second *Times* article, "Progress, They Say," appeared in the February 21, 1977, issue.

A native of Lititz, Pennsylvania, he was born in 1946 and grew up on a dairy farm. Merle and his six brothers are the sons of a Mennonite minister. Like many a youngster he wrote early and published his first poem when he was 11. While at Lancaster Mennonite High School, from which he was graduated in 1964, he wrote more poetry and added short stories and articles. He directed a teenagers' chorus assembled from

this body of citizens are uncounted numbers with writing ability. A few find their ways to religious and other writer's conferences. Others are the several persons in every community who find an outlet in being publicity and public relations committee heads, usually for women's groups. Here and there an industrious one who learned to write a little by sheer imitation manages to sell an article or short story now and then to a religious paper or magazine.

With direction and encouragement many more of these helpful and eager persons could find in religious communications an avocation; the best could fill local congregations.

After high school Merle Good was named youth secreary for the Lancaster Conference Mennonite churches, serving for two years. At the same time, beginning in 1965, he studied English and history at Eastern Mennonite College, Harrisonburg, Virginia. There he became interested in drama when he played the role of Thomas á Becket in T. S. Eliot's *Murder in the Cathedral*. The summer of 1967 was spent studying sociology in Europe. Following his marriage in 1969 to Phyllis Pellman of Millersville, Pennsylvania, he and his wife moved to New York to study at Union Theological Seminary. He obtained the master of divinity degree in 1972 with a concentration in theology and the arts. While there Good wrote radio and television scripts for the Department of Television and Radio of the New York City Council of Churches.

The Goods moved back to Lancaster County in that same year to teach writing and literature classes at Merle's old high school, Lancaster Mennonite. Two years later he left the classroom to give full attention to a business he had formed in 1970, Good Enterprises, Ltd., which he now describes as "a production company con-

permanent places in it as a vocation.

The churches might bring these potential writers to greater usefulness by sponsoring more national and regional study sessions for religious writers, by encouraging local churches to include courses in their adult education activities, and by inviting such persons to write for the church press. Much of the unsolicited copy now received is useful, to be sure, but a good deal also is useless because it is so amateurishly produced. Editors cannot afford to overlook the chance to dig out suitable contributions and to develop free-lance writers now buried in this potential mine of talent and human experience.

Merle Good

cerned with producing in the arts and providing jobs in the arts for young people (especially Mennonites)." Mr. and Mrs. Good are fulltime employees of the company.

Early in 1968 he wrote his first musical, *Strangers at the Mill,* which explored the movement of traditional Mennonites from the farm. Twenty-nine performances were given that summer in Lancaster and its author directed it. He has reported that there were "sell-out crowds of Mennonites, other local community people, and visitors to the area. It was the beginning of a tradition."

More plays followed, among them were, as he re-

The Wisdom of Specializing

Numerous books are available to help would-be freelancers learn how to assemble information, tell their stories, contract for books, build articles, market copy, and do the other work of the independent writer. Aspiring writers are often reminded that successful freelancers usually are those who specialize, as did some of those whose careers are noted briefly here. Glenn Everett draws heavily upon Washington activities; Mrs. Owens reported humorously on the homelife of a pastor's wife and then seriously on church history; Merle Good draws on the life of his own people, the Mennonites.

---

counts in an autobiographical sketch, *Who Burned the Barn Down?* (a generational struggle), *A Lot of Love* (choosing a minister by lot), *These People Mine* (a survey piece about the various Mennonite peoples), *Isaac Gets a Wife* (about a middle-aged bachelor), *Thanksgiving Day* (on the impulse to serve), *What a Peculiar People* (vignettes of the people), and *Today Pop Goes Home* (on the breakdown of the extended family).

Merle Good's first novel, *Happy as the Grass Was Green*, was published in 1970. Three years later it was made into a motion picture, *Hazel's People*, with Good as associate producer, and starring Geraldine Page and Pat Hingle.

The Dutch Family Festival, which he has produced every summer since 1970, he describes as an experiment in self-interpretation, "interpreting the spirit, faith, and culture of the Amish and Mennonites to visitors."

Embracing still another medium, Good is associate editor of the *Festival Quarterly*, a magazine published since 1974. It explores Mennonite art, religion, and culture through lively and attractive presentation. A broad venture in communications was begun in 1976 when The People's Place, of which Good is codirector, opened in Inter-

The aspiring free lance is wise to select a specialty as soon as possible and master it so that editors will look to him or her for writing on that subject. As in all other communications, free-lancing about religion is most satisfactory for the expert in the field, but much writing can be done by the well-informed lay person. Specialties are determined by what one knows most about, can learn about, or what one has natural ability for and interest in doing.

But the expert of today was not an expert from birth. This should encourage all who will take the time and do the work needed to learn techniques of communications

---

course, Pennsylvania. He writes of it as "a museum-gallery-screening room complex geared on an educational level to the expression of the arts and the search for identity among people of Anabaptist background and faith."

Merle Good's views about Christian writing appear in a lecture he gave in 1973 at Goshen College. Six temptations, he believes, beset the Christian writer. They are: (1) to not write at all because of fear of the reality of the challenge; (2) to be dishonest by covering up or ignoring the truth; (3) to not write about our own specific world, to try to write about everything out there; (4) to avoid the marketplace, "to not go into the world and let the world spit on us, on our holy things" (the church is too ingrown, speaking only to itself"); (5) to avoid critique ("a Christian must be open to critique. But a Christian when he critiques, must also be honest"); and (6) "to get caught up in our own significance.... We are not called to be great—we are called to be God's children."

On that sixth point he adds: "Perhaps I should set out to be a great writer, and you should set out to be a great whatever. I would submit that that is not Christian. The Christian is called away from that...."

and to follow the highest standards of free-lance practice.

For further reading about free-lance writing about religion:

BOOKS

Margaret J. Anderson, *The Christian Writer's Handbook*. New York: Harper & Row, 1974.

George L. Bird, *Modern Article Writing*. Dubuque, Iowa: Brown: 1967. Third edition.

Benjamin P. Browne, (ed.), *Christian Journalism for Today*. Philadelphia: Judson, 1952.

——————————, *Techniques of Christian Writing*. The same, 1960.

——————————, *The Writers' Conference Comes to You*. The same, 1956.

A. S. Burack, (ed.), *The Writer's Handbook*. Boston: The Writer, Inc. Annual.

Handbook for Christian Writers. Carol Stream, Ill.: Creation House, 1974. Sixth edition.

Helen Hull, (ed.), *The Writer's Book*. New York: Barnes & Noble, 1956.

Harry Edward Neal, *Nonfiction, from Idea to Published Book*. New York: Wilfred Funk, 1964.

——————————, *Writing and Selling Fact and Fiction*. The same, 1949.

Paul R. Reynolds, *The Writing and Selling of Non-Fiction*. Garden City, N.Y.: Doubleday, 1963.

Mildred Schell. *Wanted: Writers for the Christian Market*. Valley Forge, Pa.: Judson, 1975.

Henry F. Unger, *Writers in Roman Collars*. Fresno, Calif.: Academy Guild Press, 1959.

Roland E. Wolseley, (ed.), *Writing for the Religious Market*. New York: Association Press, 1956.

The Writer's Manual. Palm Springs, Calif.: ETC Publications, 1977.

Donald F. Yost, *Writing for Adventist Magazines*. Nashville, Tenn.: Southern Publishing Association, 1968.

Norma R. Youngberg, *Creative Techniques for Christian Writers*. Mountain View, Calif.: Pacific Press Publishing Association, 1968.

ARTICLES

See numerous articles in *The Writer* and *Writer's Digest*, both monthly magazines for free-lancers.

10 Preparing for and Starting a Career

> A statement in a book concerning the need for committed writers in this field caught my eye. For the past two years the desire to combine my Christian faith and journalism has been growing, and I realize more each day that it is in this way that I want most to communicate with people.

Thus wrote a journalism senior at a large Midwestern state university, beginning a typical inquiry about the early stages of a career in religious communications.

Other letters come from high school boys and girls as well as from men and women settled in other careers who see communications as a more effective way to serve others than what they might then be doing. A church historian, already holder of a PhD degree, switched from important teaching and administrative duties at his university, studied journalism, became a church publicist, and then moved into a major position in the religious book publishing world. A director of religious education and college religious counselor left that occupation, took another master's degree, this one in journalism, and went on to become editor of a leading children's publication for a denomination.

The question that always arises is: How should someone who wants to engage in religious communications work prepare for his or her career? Take courses in journalism? In religion? In both? In broadcasting only? In print communications only? Obtain practical experience before or after college? And where to go for such training?

As has been shown already in several of the career stories related in this book, a person does not have to be college-trained or theological-school educated to make a contribution through religious communications. But to ignore training and education for the work is to prepare the difficult way. Only a few survive under that plan, so it would seem to be the better part of wisdom to avoid it. No communicator in the religious field before the 1900s had journalism instruction because there virtually was none to be had in a formal, organized manner. But that is no reason to do without it today.

The Value of Journalistic Study

Once in a while an old-time religious journalist who did not attend a school of journalism or communications, and probably does not know how a modern one functions, poohpoohs the value of college study of the subject. But not William F. McDermott, about whose success as a free-lancer on religion we already know.

"I envy those who have the opportunity to study journalism today as a science as well as a profession," he wrote the author, "because in my day there wasn't any such thing at all, except the University of Missouri School, which was only then beginning to function."

Since the Missouri school was founded, education for journalism and communications has come to be widely accepted. Graduates of schools and departments now are among the top communicators of the nation; many thousands hold posts in all aspects of the activity.

An editor once wrote a student doing research about religious journalism that he thought the student's questionnaire placed "too much emphasis on theoretical and pedagogic instruction in this field. Bronson Alcott's dictum, 'Experience is the best teacher,' applies to journalism more definitely than in any other profession," this editor wrote.

Viewpoints like that were held by some lawyers in the days before law schools and by engineers before there were institutes of technology. That they should be held about communications in our time shows little understanding that communications has become more than a craft. In any case, aside from the fact that Alcott did not say it and Carlyle did and not in just that way, the observation is not necessarily true, for a person may gain experience but it may not be experience of the sort calculated to make him or her a competent communicator. Experience may be valuable if it is the right kind; to practice the wrong method is getting experience in it but that does not make it other than of low value. The quality of the experience is what counts, not its length or mere existence. A person who works in a magazine office for

Preparing for and Starting a Career

ten years, performing more or less the same functions all that time, is not so competent as a person who works for three years in an editorial office where he or she is given a wide variety of duties of increasing importance and difficulty and under intelligent supervision.

A well-run communications department or school provides the student with the essence of the experience he or she would obtain in many years at work. It enables the beginner to move rapidly and even to skip some unnecessary preliminaries.

Take for example the career so far of Edgar Trexler. A North Carolinian, his father was a pastor for 38 years. Edgar went from high school in North Carolina to Lenoir Rhyne College and then on to Lutheran Southern Seminary. He was ordained in 1962 by the state synod. For the next three years he was pastor of St. John's Lutheran Church in Lyons, New York, meantime taking classes at the rate of a few hours a semester for his master's in journalism, emphasizing the religious side, at Syracuse University. He was granted his degree in 1964. During those days he also free-lanced a little, placing some articles with *The Lutheran*, the biweekly of his denomination. In 1965 he joined the staff full time as an assistant editor, later being named associate editor. In time he became author of several religious books.

Edgar Trexler had had professional experience, before obtaining his degree and his place on *The Lutheran's* staff. He had edited his college and seminary papers before moving into the professional world, which was to include doing part-time work as a photographer and reporter on the Concord, North Carolina, *Daily Tribune*, and summer work on the staff of *Luther Life* magazine.

It was enough to give him a taste of the professional ways. Then his classwork equipped him to enter full-time communications on a prize-winning periodical of religion.

More than one hundred universities and colleges in the United States give degree courses in journalism and communications. Five times that number offer less than a major (eighteen or more credit hours). Quality differs

---

BIOGRAPHICAL BACKGROUND

Unsuccess Stories: Not Everyone Fulfills Hopes and Dreams

It would be unrealistic, as well as deceptive, to leave with readers of this book the impression that all who have sought careers in religious communications have achieved what they desired.

Unsuccess stories occur in all occupations; religious communications is no exception. The number of those who prepared for or attempted religious communications careers that did not materialize is undetermined. Whatever the number, the facts are that it can happen. A study of the reasons for the unhappy result would be valuable but none has been made. The reasons for failure often are unclear, in any case.

First are those, usually men because men have dominated the minority for so long, who gave up their pulpits to enter some aspect of religious communications. They write sermons and believe, therefore, that they can write other types of material, an assumption that by no means follows.

Pastor Dick Jones (not his real name) was an example. He was a hard worker but had difficulty in his postgraduate study of print journalism. Yet during his three-semester return to college he wrote freelance articles for the religious

among them; a prospective student does well to inquire about the faculty, the physical equipment for print and electronic communications, the curriculum, and the library before deciding where to go, for communications is both a technique and a social study. Generally speaking, an accredited program is to be preferred over one that is not, but some programs available have not been offered for accreditation for reasons unrelated to the quality of

---

press more successfully than most of his colleagues. After graduation, with some struggle, he found an editorial job.

A few months later he quit, sought employment elsewhere and with difficulty found it, but had to move his family clear across the continent to take it. He was severed from it in less than a year. A third post, in secular journalism this time, became available in the big city nearby, but it, too, was of short duration. Eventually he returned to the pastorate and wrote sermons again. No failure in life; by embracing a new vocation he may have shown only that one should stick to one's métier.

Why he did not make a go of it in mass communications is unclear. Perhaps it was that he was slow, too deliberate, nervous about meeting his deadlines, somewhat inflexible, and also unimaginative. These characteristics are a hindrance in many kinds of communications work.

Second is another type of communications unsuccess. It is typified by a young woman who, while introverted and shy, had talent for certain aspects of communications. She, too, planned a writing career with religion as her special area. But like Dick Jones she had trouble with the work in her classes in article writing and editing. Francine Winters (likewise not a real name) had to struggle with them because they demanded a discipline of effort she could not exhibit. She was a loner, always wanting to work on her own terms and her own schedule, a tendency

the work, such as not having the minimum number of students majoring in the subject. So far, accreditation has not been requested for a religious communications program, although preparation is available from a few institutions whose work otherwise has been highly rated.

Specific preparation in religious communications is relatively new. In the few universities that offer it the study consists largely of the core journalism and communications courses and some classes specifically in religious communications.

From 1949 to 1972 Syracuse University's School of Journalism (now renamed S. I. Newhouse School of Public Communications) maintained a subdivision of the Magazine Department to offer training in the area of religious communications. A few years after that program began, one in literacy communications was added. Both led to master's degrees. Each consisted of two special courses, Religious Writing and Religious Journalism

---

that interferes with teamwork, a growing necessity in the complex communications world.

But Fran managed to meet graduate standards and went to a job which used her major interests—graphics. She enjoyed designing page layouts and handling illustrations. Her independence, however, undid her a year or so later, for it was thought of by her church publishing house employer as uncooperativeness. She took to being a consultant in graphics and has eeked out a living at it for some years now. Her work is socially useful since she does it largely for political, social, and ethnic minorities.

But she is a far less effective person than she could be if she were willing or able to coordinate her work with that of others and with less friction.

Seminar for the first area, and Techniques of Adult Literacy and Writing for New Literates for the second. For a few terms during the 1970s a course in Religious News Writing also was offered.

All these courses rested on core programs in the major departments (newspaper, magazine, radio-television, advertising, public relations, graphic arts, and photography). Students had to complete thirty hours of graduate work and take, not for graduate credit, any non-graduate credit prerequisites to the graduate courses. All the religious and literacy journalism classes offered graduate credit.

The literacy communications courses continue, but the religious communications program was set aside in 1972 for several reasons: Lack of applicants because Syracuse, being a private university of Methodist origin, had to charge high fees; loss by resignation or retirement of several teachers who had been offering the courses; decreased support from scholarship sources; and a drop in students on in-service plans by religious publications and other offices within the church bodies.

A new master's degree program is being offered since fall, 1977, however, and called Public Communications Programs. It was originated by Professor Burton W. Marvin, assistant dean of Newhouse, teacher of several of the religious journalism courses, and one-time associate secretary, with the public relations portfolio, of the National Council of Churches. According to him it is "intended to train students for . . . general communications problems which cut across media and organizations. . . . The student following this track might be, for instance, a religious journalist interested in amplifying his (or her) other skills and research competence and returning to work in that field."

Journalism or communications was an undergraduate major at numbers of Protestant colleges in the mid-1970s. Among them are Azusa Pacific, Barrington, Bethel, Biola, Cedarville, Eastern Geneva, Grace Bible (Omaha), Grand Rapids Baptist, Hardin-Simmons, Houghton, Huntington, John Wesley, Judson, Linda Loma, Messiah Bible, Miami Christian, Pacific, Pacific Christian, Toccoa Falls, Walla Walla, Wheaton Whitnorth, and William Jewel.

A dozen or more theological seminaries offer classes in church journalism writing, publicity, or public relations, usually the latter two because they are valuable to the clergy and other church officials.

It does not follow, however, that the emphasis will be religious at any of the colleges or universities. Often giving such emphasis rests with the instructor or with the enforcement of a general policy. Because classes at Catholic colleges are permeated with religion, persons of that faith who study communications at Marquette, St. Bonaventure, Notre Dame, Fordham, and other Catholic institutions that offer degrees or majors sometimes are better prepared for religious communications than students at nonsectarian colleges that make no special point of the religious application or expect no study of religion courses.

Outside the United States standard communications programs can be found in a few regular universities of most Western nations and more so in Eastern countries. Nowhere in the world, however, are there as many degree courses and students as in the United States. The practice of preparing for a communications career in college is much less advanced elsewhere, partly because communications as a vocation does not rank as high in society. Most of the study abroad is conducted in state-operated colleges and universities; there also are a good many independent trade-school types of institutions that do not expect the student to obtain a standard liberal arts degree as well as the professional journalism study.

Religious bodies, however, have supplemented such work and developed effective offerings of their own, particularly in Africa, such as the literacy communications and publishing programs referred to in earlier chapters of this book. An example of an African center is the International Institute of Christian Communications, an activity of Daystar Communications in Nairobi, Kenya. Daystar is described as "a group of specialists in research, development, and training for effective Christian communications." The training is in-service and offered by a permanent faculty of ten, most of whom have advanced degrees from United States universities and all, except for some visiting lecturers, are Western in origin.

The courses offered are comparable in scope to those in United States programs, with adaptations to local conditions. They offer credit at Wheaton College, Western Conservative Baptist Seminary, and the School of World Missions at Fuller Theological Seminary, all American institutions.

Kinds of Study

The well-trained religious communicator has a master's degree that emphasizes the application of communications techniques to religion and a divinity school degree or a major in religion from a liberal arts college. This amount of preparation is adequate. The time is coming, however, when the doctorate will be important also because specialized knowledge in communications theory is difficult to obtain outside academic circles. Since the earlier edition of this book, more and more persons from the world of religion have obtained terminal degrees in various fields including communications. But it is not yet as generally expected as is the master's.[1]

Trained Persons Are Favored

The following question was put to 26 persons in charge of communications for a cross-section of denominations and organizations of communications in religion:

"Are there places in your organization for persons trained in communications and educated in religion? That is, is there a preference for persons with those requirements?"

All twenty-two who responded said that persons thus trained are preferred. Here are some of the answers, most are representative of the variety of replies.

Training in communications plus a good education both from seminary and practical field experience (pastoral) is a tremendous need.

—*Raymond J. Lewis*, Director, Promotion and Public Relations, American Baptist Association.

. . . yes, in our organization . . . we seem constantly in need of persons trained in communications and educated in religion. . . . Finding such people has been a major problem—especially when we need top editors.

—*Richard G. Champion* President, Evangelical Press Association, Managing Editor, *The Pentecostal Evangel*.

Preparing for and Starting a Career   205

Now it is possible in many communities to take regular college courses, to major in religion and communications, all at the same time. In an additional year the student may be able to complete the master's work, especially if he or she has an undergraduate degree in communications. The student inexperienced in or untrained for communications work may need three or four semesters for the higher degree.

Although the most proficient, systematic, and effective way is through the world of communications education,

---

In our organization we are concerned primarily with persons trained in communications. Education in religion is not necessary; however, a requirement with us would be prospects who are dedicated to the teachings of our church and who observe its standards.
—*Wendell J. Ashton*, Managing Director, Public Communications Department, The Church of Jesus Christ of Latter-day Saints.

There definitely are places in our organization for persons trained in communications and educated in religion.
—*William P. Cedfeldt*, Executive Director, Lutheran Church in America.

The NCC communications has always given preference for persons with solid theological training as well as expertise in the particular areas of communications for which they are responsible. On the other hand, we recently hired as director of Newspaper Services . . . a person who had no academic training in theology, although she had experience working with a major national denomination.
—*William F. Fore*, Assistant General Secretary for Communication, National Council of the Churches of Christ in the U.S.A.

We do . . . and periodically look for such persons as re-it is not the only way to obtain the desired training. For many years journalists and other communicators learned their occupation by being apprentices. Both secular and religious publications offices are willing to take on young people who wish to learn on the job. The young man or woman contemplating this procedure must reckon with the fact, however, that college education in general, and particularly in specialized fields, now is assumed.

Perhaps a compromise lends itself best to many per-

---

placement to current staff or as our staff expands.
—*Nelson Waybill*, Personnel Manager, Mennonite Publishing House.

The Presbyterian Church in America is favorable toward [such] persons . . . and will be seeking such persons within the next five to ten years to assist in the entire communications field.
—*Paul G. Settle*, Coordinator, Committee for Christian Education and Publications, Presbyterian Church in America.

The Mission Board . . . is indeed favorably inclined toward persons with such training. We have nearly a dozen such employees. Their responsibilities range from periodical editing to book editing to directing a news bureau to film production to mixed media educational designs to art and layout production to the operation and maintenance of electronic equipment. The most skilled . . . assist us in conceptualizing programs of interpretation, promotion, education, and communication—not only with the church constituency, but on behalf of the church with the society at large.
—*Bruce L. Robertson*, Director, Division of National Mission, Presbyterian Church in the United States.

. . . when hiring people for religious communications we would prefer to have them trained in both religion and communications. We are

Preparing for and Starting a Career

sons. When the author taught on Northwestern's and Syracuse University's downtown campuses he had in his classes men and women holding important positions on church periodicals in the Chicago and central New York areas who enrolled for one or two courses a semester, evenings only, and eventually gained their degrees. The final work was done in the last year, in residence on the main campuses, that is, in Evanston, Illinois, or Syracuse, New York. One young woman took courses in journalism

---

seldom fortunate enough to find them both together. When its necessary to make a choice, I think we prefer someone with training and experience in the area of communication where we have the need, but expect that person will be intelligent and sensitive enough to acquire knowledge of the church and a feel for the subtleties with which we work. Of course we strongly prefer someone with a Christian motivation.

—*Lois M. Joice*, Secretary for Information Services, Reformed Church in America.

There are presently about 300 public relations positions within the Southern Baptist Convention. When you include curriculum writers and journalism. These numbers editors we have around 500 professionals engaged in print have been going up at about 10 percent a year. Fortunately, we are now getting young men and women . . . trained in both communication and religion. This double-edged training and/or experience virtually doubles their chances of getting the desirable jobs.

—*Wilmer C. Fields*, Assistant to the Executive Secretary, Director of Public Relations, Southern Baptist Convention.

We prefer persons trained in communications and educated in religion, although this is a hard combination to find. We do not hold a firm stand on this.

—*Thomas D. Garner*, General Secretary, United Church Press.

at her leisure, spreading the work over ten years. Men and women, with their seminary work completed four or five years before, enrolled in Syracuse's religious journalism program, while it was available in the 1950s and 1960s, leaving their positions or obtaining a year's leave from them to make this possible. True education is never-ending; like a public school teacher, a religious journalist finds it necessary and desirable to take a class now and then; and so long-range views on the matter are the most practical. It is common for students with six to nine graduate credits in an accredited institution in their own communities to transfer them to another college elsewhere which offers the special training they desire, in this instance communications.

Before one launches on such a program, however, there should be self-examination to make sure it is likely to be effective. A rough indicator of one's capacity for work like communications is the aptitude test. Certain tests reveal literary aptitudes or vocational interests, but communications is so complex and varied that no one test is definitive. By taking general examinations it is possible to discover one's tendencies or inclinations. Information about the tests may be obtained from any vocational guidance clinic, high school, college, or university; the costs of taking them are worth it if they help to determine one's life course.

People considering religious communications as a vocation may find clues to their aptitudes for it by answering these questions about themselves:

1. Have I the same interests and abilities as persons already engaged in communications in particular?

2. Am I doing well (or did I do well) in my college

Preparing for and Starting a Career

English courses (for the writing and editing sides), accounting (and other business operations) for the management side, advertising (for that phase), and so on in other communications or related areas?

3. Are my objectives in entering religious communications not primarily self-advancement and to earn money? Do I have motives that might fairly be considered unselfish?

4. Have I sound working habits?

5. Have I a sense of vocation?

If the answers to all or most of these, especially 3 and 5, are positive one might think seriously of religious communications as a career.

Conferences, Workshops, and Volunteer Service

Several denominational, nondenominational, or interdenominational groups have established annual conferences for writers and editors; some are restricted to their own staff members.

Summer writers' and editors' conferences now are well fixed as aids to the neophyte as well as the experienced religious communicator. Several dozen are aimed at writers of any kind of material, religious or secular, fiction or nonfiction. Of special value are those intended for persons of religious interests. Various types of Lutheran, Methodist, Baptist, Church of God, Mennonite, and other denominational conferences and workshops are held, usually annually. Organizations not affiliated with any one denomination, such as the Christian Writers' Institute and *Decision* magazine, sponsor similar meetings and have done so annually for many years.

The focus of some workshops is on writing and editing

curriculum materials, but others stress poetry, the drama, or the novel. Occasionally one is devoted to religious public relations or one of its elements.

Dr. F. Donald Yost, director of archives and statistics of the General Conference of Seventh-day Adventists, himself holder of a PhD degree in communications, reports that the communications departments of his denomination's state and regional conferences "regularly conduct seminars for the communications secretaries of our local churches as well as for pastors who may be interested in attending. These seminars have to do with writing for publicity, public relations activities, and broadcasting liaison activities relating to our national radio and television broadcasts as well as local broadcasting endeavors."

Always inspirational, the more carefully organized activities of this type are helpful in transmitting technical knowledge through workshops and personal guidance. Leaders usually include prominent editors from church and secular publishing houses, professional writers of both religious and nonreligious fiction and nonfiction, and teachers of writing and communications. Writers for either children or adults, artists, and photographers also are provided with valuable short term training.

An area of service with religious communications skills which also provides coaching and experience is the Mennonite Voluntary Service Program. As described by Dale Suderman, associate director, it is "a church affiliated VISTA type program with an emphasis on collective living and service in the name of Christ."

As examples of the assignments he noted that two persons went to the staff of *Sojourners* in Washington,

D.C., working in various positions. Another volunteer was in Chicago on the staff of a Christian feminist newsletter, *Daughters of Sarah.*

This program, an agency of the General Conference Mennonite Church, consists of one, two, or three-year volunteers "who attempt to follow the radical teachings of Jesus outlined in the Sermon on the Mount." Most of the volunteers do not work in communications. But Suderman encourages persons looking for alternative careers in communications to consider contacting the MVS office. "We would be happy to work with them," he wrote to the author.[2]

Correspondence Courses

Demand for correspondence courses in religious communications is constant. None of the degree-offering universities provides such instruction in other than certain technical subjects and usually without attention to their application to religion. These subjects generally are news writing, feature and article writing, short-story writing, and a variety of composition courses, some of value to religious writers. At least two organizations, however, provide specific assistance by mail for religious writers. These are the Christian Writers' Institute, Gunderson Drive and Schmale Road, Wheaton, IL 60187, and the Christian Writers' Seminar, P.O. Box 1790, Waco, TX 76703. In 1976 the Illinois group offered five courses: Writing Techniques, Magazine Writing, Fiction Writing, Writing the Novel, and Juvenile Writing. It also sponsors annually a four-day CWI Conference and Workshop in March.

The Texas-originated Seminar puts its instructional

Job Openings Expected for the Future

Most of the heads of communications offices of denominations, church publishing houses, religious communications organizations, and other bodies, when asked late in 1976, "Do you expect to have openings for personnel in the next five years or so in your communication work?" answered positively. Typical replies are those below. On a positive or negative scale they came to 18 positive, 4 negative. Twenty-seven were asked the question; 22 responded.

... there are limited opportunities from time-to-time
—*James Z. Nettinga*, Information Department, National Division, American Bible Society.

... Openings will be occasional at best, and virtually all will be at the diocesan level.
—*John C. Goodbody*, Executive for Communication, Executive Council for the Episcopal Church.

... I would expect continuing growth in evangelical publishing which would mean additional openings for trained journalists in the next five years or so.
—*Richard G. Champion*, President, Evangelical Press Association.

I'm sure there will be openings in the next five years in

---

materials on ten cassettes, dividing them into eight sessions, with such titles as Basic Rules for Writing, What the Editor Wants, Tools for Writing, Writers Who Are Successful, Specialty Writing, and Getting Your Manuscript Published. The plan is an enterprise of Word Books, a Texas religious book publishing house.

The advertising columns of magazines for writers, *The Writer* and *Writer's Digest* in particular, and for literary people generally, such as the small literary magazines, carry announcements of a wide range of conferences, workshops, and courses of varied quality. Most of them

Preparing for and Starting a Career 213

many areas of our denomination. . . .
—*George L. Ford*, Director, Information and Stewardship, The Free Methodist Church.

Yes, we expect openings. . . . We foresee openings for persons trained with the electronic media and in public relations work generally.
—*Wendell J. Ashton*, Managing Director, Public Communications Department, The Church of Jesus Christ of Latter-day Saints.

. . . we definitely will have openings . . . on both the editor level and in the field of radio, TV, etc.
—*William P. Cedfeldt*, Executive Director, Office for Communications, Lutheran Church in America.

No, I do not expect any openings for additional personnel.
—*Raymond J. Lewis*, Director, Promotion and Public Relations, Baptist Sunday School Committee, American Baptist Association.

Such openings . . . will be dictated solely by the fluctuations of our budget. . . . The encouraging word, however, is that more and more opportunities will be opening up for specialists in religious communications at the regional and community level.
—*Bruce L. Robertson*, Director, Division of National Mission, Presbyterian Church in the United States.

I would certainly feel that

are for the commercial writer, although some are useful to religious writers. A prospective student should check their comparative cost, the reputations of the teachers actually handling the manuscripts and dealing with the writer, and the scope of the instruction. Conferences for secular writers mainly sometimes are attended by persons with codes of conduct offensive to the religious writer; it is wise to inquire of experienced teachers about the social activities at conferences.

Like schools and departments of communications, correspondence courses can teach some of the craft of writ-

we would have such expectation. Our publications are issued from a National Publications Department, and the editor-in-chief is continually on the alert for suitable, qualified personnel. . . . Across the USA there will doubtless be many opportunities for persons qualified in public relations. Further . . . we are often looking for qualified secretaries who, in addition to secretarial skills, have some creative ability in Christian education and some training in journalism.
—*Colonel George Nelting,* National Chief Secretary, The Salvation Army.

. . . yes . . . let me report a step that we have taken forward that will help make these openings possible. . . . 1976 marked the first year of a communication internship program comparable to the ministerial internships of our church. . . . In 1977 there will be six more. . . .
—*M. Carol Hetzell,* Director, Department of Communication, General Conference of Seventh-day Adventists.

At the moment and in the foreseeable future we have no openings in publication.
—*Thomas D. Garner,* General Secretary, United Church Press.

---

ing but not the art. A writer with nothing to say and little native ability can take courses all his or her life and never be more than a hack.

It should be remembered that communications techniques can best be learned by performing them under circumstances as nearly like reality as possible. Courses by mail provide no opportunity for discussion, make only limited use of library and research methods, and are impersonal. They should be taken if residence instruction is impossible to obtain and for the inspiration and discipline they provide. A writer who must have a deadline to make him or her work will find a well-organized correspondence course an incentive.

We do have an advertising department which does have openings from time to time. Currently we are without a book editor and there will be an upcoming decision on this.... We usually are hard pressed to find suitably trained persons....
—*Harold L. Phillips*, Editor in Chief, Warner Press.

... we have a constant need for people who are professionals in the area of journalism particularly; not so much in the media of radio and television, because our production is done through agencies. Nearly all of our departments ... oriented to church ministries are in need of people in journalism.
—*Lee Shultz*, National Director, Division of Communications. The Assemblies of God.

We expect to have a number of openings for personnel in the communication system of the denomination in the next five years. The communications people will need to have a variety of skills and specialties, from journalists to film writers to producers to public relations people.
—*Nelson Price*, Director, Public Media Division. United Methodist Church.

Scholarships, Fellowships, and Assistantships

A talented and dedicated person may be prevented from obtaining the needed special training by inability to pay the constantly rising fees needed by the institutions that offer preparation for religious communications careers. Scholarships and other financial aids have been the solution for some persons, young or even those already launched in their work.

Although few of the aids available are indicated as being for any phase of religious communications, students at the graduate level will find that they may, under some circumstances, study religious communications as their specialties. Ministerial dependent scholarships also are available at some church-related colleges.

To obtain detailed information applicants should read carefully the references to scholarships, fellowships, and assistantships in the catalogs of the institutions they wish to attend. They also should consult the books summarizing these opportunities; one or more of these can be found at public libraries and at academic and school counseling offices and libraries. Inquiries should be made at denominational offices. The Newspaper Fund, Inc., annually issues a "Journalism Scholarship Guide" available from the Fund at Box 200, Princeton, NJ 08540, or from the American Council on Education for Journalism, School of Journalism, University of Missouri, Columbia, MO 56201; the latter also will send a list of accredited programs in communciations.

Grants differ in amounts as well as in requirements and advantages. A fellowship or assistantship requires the holder to do a certain number of hours of work each week or term. It may be research, teaching, or some less responsible duty, depending upon the applicant's experience and abilities.[3]

Organizations in Religious Communications

Although religious communications is numerically a small occupation, those who practice it are not alone, for there are various organizations which they join for fellowship, inspiration, exchange of shop talk, professional advancement, encouragement, and even for refresher courses. Church and religion news writers and editors for the secular press have their Religion Newswriters Association (RNA). Editors and publishers of Protestant religious newspapers and magazines have

Preparing for and Starting a Career

Officers of the Associated Church Press in a recent year; left to right, top row: James Hawkinson (Covenant Companion), Dennis Shoemaker, executive secretary, ACP; and C. Ray Dobbins (Cumberland Presbyterian), president, ACP. Bottom row; Howard Royer (Messenger) and Betty Gray (then of Episcopal New Yorker).

two national groups, the Associated Church Press (ACP) and the Evangelical Press Association (EPA). Religious publicity and public relations workers assemble nationally once a year and regionally at least monthly through the Religious Public Relations Council (RPRC). A few denominations have their own press associations, among the larger and more active (often in cooperation with ACP) are the Catholic Press Association (CPA), the Southern Baptist Press Association (SBPA), and the American Jewish Press Association (AJPA), although the latter does not consider itself a group of religious communicators so much as an organization of community newspaper editors.

Religious communications in the United States lacks a publication to serve all the persons engaged in this work, the result of its denominational and occupational segmentation. The publications for these partitions include *The Catholic Journalist,* the *News Letter* of the Religion Newswriters Association, the Associated Church Press *Newsletter* (formerly *Dynamic* and *Copy Log*), *The Christian Author* issued for students of the Christian Writers Institute, the newsletter of the Religious Public Relations Council, the *FCAME Newsletter* issued by the Fellowship of Christians in the Arts, Media, and Entertainment, and sundry other much smaller newssheets produced by community or regional groups for members of some of these national organizations. *Action,* the newsletter of the World Association for Christian Communications, although published in London, has information about developments in the United States as well as other nations. The *WACC Journal* is a quarterly magazine and carries more in-depth material than *Action,* such as full-length articles discussing issues in religious communications.

Teaching Religious Communications

Walter Wiebe, a Canadian Mennonite religious journalist whose death as a young man in 1962 saddened his colleagues, wrote an editorial for the *Religious Journalism Newsletter* in which he likened religious journalism to marriage.

"Personally," he wrote, "I believe in religious

journalism, as I believe in love and marriage. To say that religion and journalism cannot mix is like saying John and Mary cannot get married because John is a man, and Mary—well, she is a lady. But what will you say when John and Mary fall in love? They *will* go to church and get married—as religion and journalism have done. I would not like to see them take the road to Reno."

The satisfaction that Walter Wiebe took in the union of religion and journalism makes an appeal to the teacher of the subject of religious communications. If practicing religious communications is a form of evangelism or mission work, certainly helping to train those who will do such work offers rewards beyond those ordinarily experienced by a teacher of some less dynamic subject.

Opportunities to do such teaching remain small. The demand for courses is modest. The need for teachers will increase only as enrollments for such classes rise in the colleges, universities, and seminaries. Most instruction has been left to regular faculty members who happened to have experience in this special field or the personal interest to attempt such courses. As with religious communications itself, what is required is the personal dedication, the knowledge of a special vocabulary and background, and a motivation different from that of the secularist.

Some of the persons who have provided notable professional services during this century as teachers of religious communications or regular courses with a religious emphasis include:

William F. Tanner, Oklahoma Baptist University
DeWitt C. Reddick, University of Texas

Floyd Baskette, University of Colorado
Robert W. Root, Syracuse University
Robert S. Laubach, Syracuse University
Richard T. Baker, Columbia University
Ralph B. Churchill, Southwest Baptist Theological Seminary
G. S. Dobbins, Southern Baptist Theological Seminary
Fred Eastman, Chicago Theological Seminary
Frank E. Burkhalter, Baylor University
C. S. Bryant, Baylor University
Roberta Moore, Walla Walla and Linda Loma Colleges
Webb Garrison, Scarritt College and Emory University
Miron A. Morrill, Cornell College
John E. Drewry, University of Georgia
Ira L. Baker, Furman University and High Point College
John De Mott, Northern Illinois University and Temple University
John Charles Wyn, Colgate-Rochester Divinity School
James W. Carty, Jr., Bethany College
James Foltz, Penn State University

Dr. De Mott's background indicates the kind a layperson might bring to teaching religious communications. Like most such educators, he teaches both religious and secular journalism simultaneously.

Dr. De Mott went from fifteen years in communications work into teaching in 1962. A Kansan by birth, he was educated at Kansas City Junior College, the University of Kansas, the University of Missouri, and Northwestern University, from the latter earning a PhD in mass communications in 1971.

His practical experience includes being a reporter for the Kansas City *Star,* a leading daily, covering a variety of beats, including sports, public affairs, and crime.

When he shifted to teaching, he was city desk assignment editor at the *Star*.

Before going to Temple, Dr. De Mott was on the faculties of the William Allen White School of Journalism at the University of Kansas, the Medill School of Journalism at Northwestern University, and the department of journalism at Northern Illinois University.

At the latter he launched the Interpretation of Religion News Project, a program of specialized graduate study linked with the university's regular communications course work. When he left NIU the project was discontinued. At this writing, however, he expected to develop a new plan at Temple, which, being in Philadelphia, has great possibilities of receiving local support.

Other of his activities related to preparation for the religious communications field include membership on the national committee of professional standards of the Associated Press Managing Editors Association, serving on a subcommittee that prepared the code of ethics for managing editors. He was coeditor of *The Journalist's Prayer Book* and has conducted seminars and workshops for religious journalists. He was a correspondent for Religious News Service while in news work in Kansas.

Among his students have been a number who went into religious journalism. A few are Bruce Even, news director of a Christian radio station in Rockford, Illinois; Danute Tiskus, a broadcast news media liaison aide at the office of information, Chicago Catholic Chancery; Carol Fouke, religion news editor, The Rockford Newspapers, Rockford, Ill.; Margaret Cathcart Clark and Leta Cathcart Roth, both religion news editors, for the Kansas

City *Kansan*, Kansas; and James Robison, religion news editor, Chicago *Tribune*.

Jim Robison did his former teacher proud by winning the Supple Award for 1976, the high honor conferred on one of the members of the Religion Newswriters Association each year.

Religious communications, technically speaking, is not different enough from any other types to require extensive religious training by someone who presumes to teach it. Thus a competent communications instructor who has been active in his church or temple becomes familiar with the special differences between secular and religious journalism, is sincerely devoted to that faith, is experienced in secular and religious communications professionally, and is knowledgeable generally about religion, may obtain an opportunity to educate young people for a career in religious communications.

Earning a Living in Religious Communications

"Religious journalism has been an honor without profit," said Dr. Peter Gordon White, for many years editor of the United Church of Canada's church school publications and its educational literature. He used a tense of the past, but considerable truth still rests in his statement even though conditions are improving.

Yet we must face the fact that no one ever becomes rich in the communications work of the religious world. If getting rich or famous is of concern, the person does not belong in religious journalism or communications. An individual's fame or achievement of wealth is not the goal of such work.

But now, more than ever, it is possible to earn a decent

Preparing for and Starting a Career 223

living in this phase of communications; if one is especially gifted and industrious it is possible to do even better. Hundreds of persons who help edit or manage church magazines, work as religion news writers and editors, or do some of the other tasks already described, own their own homes, support families, and enjoy the other benefits of middle-class America. But not the beginner, usually. Beginners ordinarily must start comparatively low, as in any occupation. And just as in secular communications, there are some institutions that underpay people, although they are few in the religious field.

Religious communication's best organizations pay salaries comparable to those of other publications, public relations, publicity, news bureau, syndicate, and broadcasting offices of similar size, circulation, or range. Since all are small rather than large, however, this means that salaries may be in the lower brackets in any national comparison.

Any communicator is mistaken if he judges an occupation by its raw salary figures. Compare these situations, for example:

Employee A, Institution A, State A	*Employee B, Institution B, State B*
Base annual salary—$12,000	Base annual salary—$10,000
Social Security—is eligible	Social Security—is eligible
Group life insurance—obtainable	Group life insurance—obtainable
State income tax averages $260	State income tax—none
Annual average transportation expenses—$250	Transportation cost—none (resides near office)
Cost of Living differential with Employee B—$710	Group medical insurance—available

Group medical insurance—not available

Free-lance earnings—not permitted or impractical

Free-lance earnings—average $800 annually

Employee B, judged on base salary alone, is earning $2,000 less than A. The cash earnings are really only $1,200 less. And B's benefits are greater by far than A's, and the fixed charges much lower. It costs A $1,150 more than it does B to pay rent and food costs because A lives where prices are higher. B lives so close to the job that B can walk (or neighbors or co-workers take B to the office or shop). A must pay cash for transportation. In the final analysis B's take-home pay actually is several hundred dollars higher than A's. Other facts to be considered seriously are opportunities for promotion, nearness to church and school, nature of housing, and other intangibles not measurable in dollars.

Scales of payment for full-time employees are far better in religious communications than are the rates paid free-lance writers of religious materials. These rates always have been low but some are improving. Denominational magazines are likely to pay from $15 to $50 for an article, occasionally $100 and rarely $200 and $300. (The highest usual rates in secular periodicals are $3,000, with occasional figures far higher for star writers.) Editors or their boards of control have been slow to raise rates for free-lanced copy partly through inability, partly because the field is crowded with would-be writers, and partly because of a desire to offset appallingly climbing production costs. Some offices are raising rates gradually.

Common rates for free-lance material range about as follows:

Articles and stories for adult periodicals . . . ½¢ to 10¢ a word
Fiction for story papers . . . . ½¢ to 5¢ a word
Articles, departmental material for story papers.
¼¢ to 5¢ a word
Devotional materials . . . . ½¢ to 1¢ a word
Poetry . . . . 14¢ to $1 a line
Photographs (black and white) . . . . $1 to $25 a print
Photographs (transparencies) . . . . $25 to $100 each

Additional earnings are possible through sale of second or simultaneous rights. Since religious publications usually are noncompeting (Baptists do not read Methodist publications and the like) editors are willing to allow writers to resell material to other publications at a lower fee with the understanding that the first purchaser has right to first publication. More and more are agreed, under the same principle of noncompetition, that writers may submit material simultaneously to numerous editors. In both situations all editors are informed of the plan.

Religious publishing houses also long have had the practice, often desirable, of paying a flat sum for a typescript or other material instead of a royalty, as on books. The risk with religion is greater than with most secular material, and this policy assures the writer or artist of a fair return for the work.

But religious publishers have not yet solved the problem of paying adequately those free-lancers who wish to make a living entirely from writing. A clergyman, teacher, or some other fully employed person who writes on the side is less injured by moderate rates for part-time work than is a writer trying to live entirely by the typewriter. Editors and publishers and others in the religious world who buy material from communicators are showing more and more appreciation of well-prepared material useful to them.

In the religious field editors have the opportunity to improve other writer-editor relationships of which beginners should be aware. Many editors are slow to read, accept, reject, and pay for typescripts; some are unbusinesslike in their correspondence. So many executives must spend so much time on other duties that they cannot do their editorial work as efficiently as they may desire; often they are public speakers, travelers, board secretaries, or are pastors, priests, or rabbis, with all or most of the duties of the clergy. In times of economic duress, as in the mid-1970s, staffs are reduced and duties added to the survivors of budget cuts.

Truly dedicated missionary communicators never would become such if money were of much importance to them. They enter this aspect of religious communications with a faith and a spirit beyond the capacities of men and women who measure success in dollars and cents. Often lovably quixotic, they hold to a philosophy that nevertheless comes closest to that sacrificial attitude needed of all persons if the kingdom of God is to become a reality on earth.

Sincere missionaries in a foreign field desire to be inconspicuous, to live as do the people with whom they work, and to be unostentatious. Their needs therefore are limited and their salaries can be modest by comparison with what is paid religious communicators who must work under the costly conditions of life in the United States and many other Western nations.

Deprivation, not only of many of the creature comforts

Dr. A. K. John, second from right, a literacy leader in India, is shown here with Dr. Robert S. Laubach (first, right) at a literacy class near Kathikappally, Kerala.

of American life but also of the cultural advantages, appears in many instances to be the price of missionary existence. This deprivation is experienced joyfully by some missionaries as part of their service and their defiance of mortal dependence upon the present world. Young people who look forward to this field should realize that they will have little money to spare for luxuries.

Unions in Religious Communications

Anyone conscious of the part of trade unionism in modern life may wonder if it enters the field of religious communications. It does, in two ways, and thus has an effect upon the problem of earning a living in this occupation. An undetermined number of religious publishing houses, or the printing and other production and processing firms they engage if they do not have their own facilities, have contracts with unions on the mechanical side. Men and women who are religious news editors or writers for secular journalism may be employed by companies with similar contracts and themselves are sometimes members of the American Newspaper Guild, an AFL-CIO union, of reporters, copyeditors, accountants, and other below-executive class employees. Most major dailies, the large news agencies and broadcasting companies, and a few magazines have contracts with the Guild.

Under pressure from persons who believe that living the social gospel logically means support of trade unionism, church publishers that own their own plants but do not have union contracts with their employees have been put to a test and have been asked for explanations. The

Preparing for and Starting a Career

issue has been placed before employees, the publishers explain, and the employees have voted down union affiliation because, in some instances, their pay scales, pension plans, and other benefits would be diminished rather than enhanced by union affiliation.

The benefits and obligations of trade unionism, therefore, are not obligatory or even available to every religious communicator. It depends upon where the individual works.

Secretarial Work as an Entry

In religious communications men and women hold about the same jobs at the lower and middle areas of the ladder, with some exceptions. But at the upper extremity the field always has been dominated by men, and only now are women beginning to achieve top positions, particularly in the administrative area. This situation has its parallel in the secular communications arena.

For only one reason might men be separated from women in a discussion of religious communications as a vocation: the fact that women have the traditional field of secretarial work as a means of entry into the field. But it is one they rarely are enthusiastic about.

Women educated for communications usually shy away from secretarial training, declaring that if they have it they will forever be stuck in a stenographic job and never have a chance to write, edit, or hold some other editorial responsibility. They say this the June they are graduated, but by the following June they confess in letters to former teachers that they were foolish. They urge the current crop of girl graduates to learn shorthand and typing pronto. They never reveal, however, just what the professors can do to make the new group of girl students believe what the earlier group refused to accept as truth.

And it is the truth. Though demands in these for capable young people have dropped somewhat, there still are many opportunities, as the results of a survey displayed in chapter 10 indicate. That small test of the field does not take in the opportunities in the foreign field.

The objectives should be to find the right position, unless starvation looms. Sometimes it is wiser to begin as a quasi secretary-editorial employee in an office that will provide opportunities to do important writing or editorial or publicity work later than to begin as an assistant editor in a situation where there is little or no possibility for greater usefulness or growth.

The young woman of editorial, literary, or some other communications talent soon will be appreciated and taken from behind the shorthand notebook or some mechanical office device to do the more difficult work on the editorial desk, with cameras, or whatever else is needed for production of whatever communications materials are the responsibility of the particular office. Few employers are so foolish as to overlook the creative ability in communications when it is so greatly needed by all the media at work in the world of religion.

Distinction should be made, also, between *secretaries* and *stenographers*, worthy as each person may be. An editor's secretary, for instance, often knows more about the publication's operations than anyone else, including the topmost executive. It is not uncommon for a secretary to become an officer of a church publishing house or public relations office. First-rate secretaries are better paid and more valuable than some assistant or associate editors, staff writers, or others who have limited knowledge of the total operation.

Getting the Job

The first step, beyond training and education, in earning a living at religious communications, is finding a job. Advice on job getting could fill another book the size of this one. The principles are the same as for any other occupation except for a few details.

When applying for a secular position one's religious affiliation need not be mentioned, for the decision to hire should be made without reference to the applicant's church connection; to do otherwise is to discriminate. But the religious institution naturally wants and needs to know about an applicant's churchlife, for it is relevant.

If applicants make personal calls on possible employers they should use common sense about their appearance, correct any bad personal habits, and refrain from doctrinal disputes. They may make clear their theological positions, if asked, or even if not, lest they be hired under a misapprehension. A communicator who doubts that the Bible is entirely an inspired document should avoid offices that function on the assumption that it is.

A data sheet, that is a résumé, dossier, or other biographical compilation, should be prepared for any extensive mailing of applications for jobs. This sheet should be accompanied by a brief personal letter. For communications, especially, a data sheet that is merely a chronological list of educational and employment highlights is unimpressive. It should itself be attractively written, edited, and designed. Both sheet and covering letter should be prepared meticulously, free of misspellings and errors of statement, and couched in clear English. A stamped, return envelope should be included; if for overseas, enclose an International Reply Coupon, available at post offices.

Because religious publications are rarely on general newsstands, job applicants must do library work and use letters to assemble a proper mailing or calling list. Some religious publications, public relations offices, and other places to work may be included in the usual directories, but most are not. When ready to start compiling a list the applicant might consult these reference sources:

Ayer Directory of Publications. Philadelphia, Pa.: N.W. Ayer & Son, Inc. Annual.
Handbook for Christian Writers. Carol Stream, Ill.: Creation House, 1974.
The Literary Market Place. New York: R. R. Bowker & Co. Annual.
The Writer's Handbook. Boston: The Writer, Inc., Annual.
The Writer's Market. Cincinnati, Ohio: Writer's Digest. Annual.
Editor & Publisher International Year Book. New York: *Editor & Publisher Magazine.* Annual.
Year Book of American and Canadian Churches. Nashville, Tenn.: Abingdon Press, Annual.
Standard Periodical Directory. New York: Oxbridge, 1977.

As this book is being written it is reported that a databank, "with information on thousands of communication specialists around the world," was being set up in California by an organization known as Resources for Communication. The owner of the system is Robert F. Cramer, a one-time editor of religious periodicals and publicists for religious groups, himself a holder of degrees in communications with a stress on religious application.

The system is called PAGE, meaning Persons and Groups Everywhere, and was expected to provide communicators' names and addresses, samples or information about their work, and their backgrounds and special areas of interest and expertise.

If this plan becomes successful, it will be a valuable clearinghouse for job seekers and employers in religious communications. Executive secretaries of such groups as EPA, ACP, RPRC, and others listed in this book may know of openings as do schools of journalism and communications, especially those that prepare persons for the religious field. Applicants have found it worthwhile to send letters and dossiers to their alma maters as well as to professional associations. Registering with employment agencies is helpful.

The Denominational Fences

Denominationalism is a handicap as well as an advantage to employer and employee alike. The way it is a handicap is reflected in a letter from a publishing house. Its advertising manager wrote for the names of graduating students who might be copywriters. The manager pointed out that he wanted "a person who has imagination enough to see the needs a book or church supply item will fill, and who is able to describe his product with the ring of the genuine in his words."

His organization, he explained, issues more than seventy periodicals, operates about forty bookstores, and has a publishing house issuing from 35 to 40 books a year.

Millions of pieces of direct mail are produced annually by this institution.

The letter also said:

"Due to our major audience, he (or she) must be a member of a _____ church."

This restriction had the virtue, at least, of reducing the competition for the job. By and large such a restriction holds, but it is less often insisted upon. During the same week that this inquiry arrived there came, from the editor of a rapidly growing denominational weekly, an inquiry for a young Protestant journalist to be an assistant editor. No denomination was specified as imperative.

The director of a large office handling publicity for a mission board at about the same time wrote the author for suggestions of persons who might be available to join his staff as an executive. He explained that he was not fussy about denomination, although he preferred to have someone in sympathy with the work of the board.

There are Protestants and Protestants, just as there are Jews and Jews and Catholics and Catholics. Obviously someone who is conservative theologically and takes his or her religious philosophy seriously and literally would be restive and unhappy on the staff of a so-called liberal or modernist publication, and vice versa. But there are enough publications of all persuasions to provide varied outlets.

Also, it should be remembered that a person working for the magazine or publicity office of some denomination other than his or her own is likely never to become head of the division unless he or she forsakes the original affiliation. In these days of frequent mergers this risk is not so great as once it was, at least in Protestantism. The growth of ecumenism in the whole world of religion is favorable to this aspect of religious communications.

For more information about preparing for and starting the career see:

BOOKS

Herbert Brucker, *Journalist*. New York: Macmillan, 1962. Chapter 11, "How Do I Get In?"

Ira Henry Freeman and Beatrice O. Freeman. *Careers and Opportunities in Journalism*. New York: Dutton, 1966. Chapter 4, "The Opportunities and Pay," Chapter 12, "Newspaper Working Conditions and Pay," Chapters 22 and 23, "Getting Started in Journalism."

Norman M. Lobsenz, *Writing as a Career*. New York: Walck, 1963. Chapter 12, "How to Prepare for a Writing Career."

Leonard Ames Ryan and Bernard Ryan, Jr., *So You Want to Go into Journalism*. New York: Harper & Row, 1963. Chapter 3, "The First Steps."

Arville Schaleben, *Your Future in Journalism*. New York: Richards Rosen, 1961. Chapter 18, "Self Evaluation: How to Apply."

Marion Sitzmann and Reloy Garcia, *Successful Interviewing*. Skokie, Ill.: National Textbook, 1976.

M. L. Stein, *Your Career in Journalism*. New York: Messner, 1965. Chapter 2, "Start Preparing Now."

Roland E. Wolseley, *Understanding Magazines*. Ames: Iowa State University Press, 1969. Second edition. Chapter 24, "Breaking into the Magazine World."

ARTICLES AND PAMPHLETS

Freeman H. Betts, "Careers for Those Who Are

Interested in English, Languages, and Journalism." Education Commission, Southern Baptist Convention. (Pamphlet.)

Bert N. Bostrom, "How to Apply for a Job in Media." *The Quill*, October 1976.

James W. Carty, Jr., "Careers in Religious Journalism." *Christian Action*, July 1958.

Church Occupations and Voluntary Service. Nashville, Tenn.: Board of Higher Education and Ministry, United Methodist Church, 1976. (Pamphlet.)

J. Daniel Hess, "Attitudes Toward Journalism in Church-Related Colleges." *Journalism Quarterly*, Spring 1963. See also *Moody Monthly*, March 1976 and March 1977.

Robert W. Root, "Career Opportunities in Religious Journalism." Board of Education, The Methodist Church, and the Methodist Publishing House, 1965. (Pamphlet.)

James G. Saint, Jr., "Cameras Click for Christ." *This Day*, July 1962.

F. Donald Yost, "Leaders of Thought." *The Youth's Instructor*, November 14, 1967.

NOTES

1. Under the heading, "Ministries in Communication," the United Methodist Church Board of Higher Education and Ministry suggests the kind of preparation needed for religious journalism as a vocation. It is a small paperback. See *Church Occupations and Voluntary Service* in reading list below.

2. Mennonite Voluntary Service is at 722 Main St., Newton, KS 67114.

3. The Evangelical Press Association provides at least two $500 scholarships a year to college students contemplating careers in Chris-

tian communications. The Ralph Stoody Fellowship of $3,000 is offered annually by the United Methodist Church and several scholarships are offered by Laubach Literacy, Inc. The latter, known as the Laubach Literacy and Mission Fund Scholarships at Syracuse University, are annual.

Index

Abbot, Willis J., 94
Allen, Devere, 180
American Jewish Press Association, 217
American Newspaper Guild, 228, 229
Anderson, Margaret, 181
Armstrong, Marjorie Moore, 181-184
Artists, 56-57
Ashton, Wendell J., quoted, 62, 205, 213
Associated Church Press, 217
Associated Negro Press, 122
Associated Press, 52

Baehr, Ann Elizabeth: see Price, Ann Elizabeth
Baker, David D., 172
Baker, Helen E., 38
Baker, Ira L., 220
Baker, Richard T., 220
Barrett, Lois Y., 98-100
Baskette, Floyd, 220

Bernstein, Carl, 91
Block, Lillian R., 74, 95, 96-101, 160
Bolles, Donald, 132
Bontrager, Robert, 146-147
Book publishing, 55-56
Briscoe, Sherman, 83
Browne, Benjamin P., 101
Brummitt, Dan B., 101
Bryant, C. E., 133, 220
Buckner, George Walker, Jr., 38, 101
Burbank, Peter, 53
Burkhalter, Frank E., 220
Byrd, Annie Ward, quoted, 35

Cadigan, Robert J., 38, 95, 96
Campbell, Benjamin P., 104-106
Canham, Erwin H., 39, 94
Carty, James W., Jr., 26-27, 32-33, 35-38, 74
Cassells, Louis, 74
Catholic Press Association, 163, 217
Cedfelt, William P., quoted, 205, 213

Champ, Isabel, 182-184
Champion, Richard G., quoted, 61, 204, 212
Christian Century, 94
Christian Science Monitor, The, 94, 102
Christian Herald Association, 93
Christian Writers' Institute, 209-211
Christian Writers' Seminar, 211
Christianity and democracy, 18-19
Church school literature, 57-59
Churchill, Ralph B., 220
Churchman, The, 95
Clark, Dennis, 152
Coates, Fletcher, 39
Cogley, John, 39, 74
Colligan, James P., 156-167
Commonweal, 94
Communications:
    characteristics, 15-18
    charges against, 59-62
    definitions, 14, 26
    education for, 195-209
    literacy, 141, 144-150
    power of, 16-17, 21-23
    teaching, 218-222
Communications Recruitment and Training, Inc., 115
Communicators, 58-59
Conferences, 209-211
Cooper, Dave, 79-81
Cornell, George W., 74
Correspondence courses, 211-214
Cowan, Loretta, 84
Cramer, Robert F., 232, 233
Crawford, Robert, 146, 148
Culver, Elsie, 38
Curriculum writing, 58-59

Daniels, George M., 122-123
Davis, Melodie Miller, 53
Daystar Communications, 138-139, 203
De Mott, John, 220-222
Deseret News, The, 102
Dick, LaVernae, 186-187
Dinwoodie, William, 74
Dobbins, C. Ray, 217
Draib, Dorothy A., 84
Drewry, John E., 220
Drury, Barbara, 84
Dudde, William A., 141-142
Dugan, George, 39, 74-75

Eastman, Fred, 220
Eby, Omar, 150
Eby, Paul, 38
Ehrensperger, Harold A., 101
Elfers, Robert A., 95-96
Eshenaur, Ruth, 137-141, 154
Ethics, 108-109
Evangelical Literature Overseas, 149-150
Evangelical Press Association, 217
Everett, Glenn D., 172-174

Fairfield, James G., 53
Fees, 224, 225
Fellowship of Christians in the Arts, Media, and Entertainment, 218
Ferrari, Erma Paul, quoted, 21
Ferren, J. K., 126
Ferrer, Terry, 74
Fey, Harold, 38, 94
Fields, Wilmer C., quoted, 11, 39, 63, 207
Folger, William, 74
Ford, George L., quoted, 213
Fore, William F., quoted, 205
Foltz, James, 220
Fortson, John L., 132
Fry, Harrison W., 39, 74
Frakes, Margaret, 94

Gammon, Roland S., 132
Garner, Thomas D., quoted, 63, 207, 214
Garrison, Webb, 171-172, 220
Geier, Woodrow A., 132
Geyer, Alan, 94
Good, Merle, 186-191

Index

Goodbody, John C., quoted, 61, 212
Gray, Betty, 217
Gray, Helen Gott, 75, 83
Groesbeck, Marian W., 110-112

Hall, Clarence, 93, 95, 96
Harrington, Janette, 39
Hartnett, Robert C., 101
Haselden, Kyle, 94
Hawkinson, James, 217
Heatwole, Larry, 53
Henry, Carl F. H., 39
Hess, Doris, 146-148
Hetzell, M. Carol, quoted, 63, 214
Hosie, Laurence, quoted, 111-113
Hoyt, Robert, 38
Hutchinson, Paul, 38, 101
Hyer, Marjorie, 75

Intermedia, 149
International Institute of Christian Communications, 138-139, 203
Irion, Mary Jean, 184

Jackson, Birdie M., 83
Job-getting, 231-233
John, A. K., 227
Johnson, Edna Ruth, 95
Johnson, Jim, 152
Joice, Lois M., quoted, 207
Journalism's scope, 17-18

Kinsolving, Lester, 75
Klausler, Alfred M., 39

Laubach, Frank C., quoted, 141, 142, 178
Laubach, Robert S., 142, 143, 144-147, 220, 227
Lewis, Raymond Jr., quoted, 61, 204, 213
Lindsey, Gordon R., 131
Lipphard, William B., 39, 101
Lutheran, The, 94, 95

Macdonald, Clifford P., 131

Marvin, Burton W., 201, 202
Maryknoll, 157, 160-161
McClellan, Albert, 133
McCorkle, Henry L., 38-39
McCoy, Robbie L., 83
McDermott, William F., quoted, 66-67; 174-176
McDowell, Rachel, 79
McKee, William T., quoted, 61
Martin, Harold E., 88-89
Marty, Martin E., 94
Mass communications defined, 14
Media defined, 17
Mennonite Broadcasts, Inc., 53
Methodist Information, 129
Minorities, 82-84
Minsky, Louis, 97
Missionary Tidings, 112
Modean, Erik W., 39, 133
Moore, Alfred D., 152
Moore, Roberta, 220
Morrill, Miron A., 220
Morrison, Charles Clayton, 94
Moseley, Louise, 39
Moyer, Marie, quoted, 153
Murch, James DeForest, 101
Murray, Virgie W., 83

Nall, T. Otto, 101
Nannes, Caspar, 39, 75, 77
National Catholic News Service, 92
National Council of Churches of Christ in the U.S.A., 51
National Courier, 102
Nelting, George, quoted, 62, 214
Nettinga, James Z., quoted, 212
News for You, 145-146
News World, The, 102
Nichol, Francis D., 101
Norman, Lynn, 83
Norton, William Bernard, 73-74

Ostling, Richard, 75
Organizations, 216
Owens, Loulie Latimer, 181

Parker, Everett, 39; quoted, 63; 113, 116
Paye, Anne, 127-128
Philbrick, Richard B., 75
Phillips, Harold L., quoted, 215
Phillips, McCandlish, 76-77
Photographers, 56-57
Poling, Dan A., 93, 101
Peerman, Dean, 94
Price, Ann Elizabeth, 75, 79-82
Price, Jo-ann: see Price, Ann Elizabeth
Price, Nelson, quoted, 62, 215
Promotion defined, 121
Press agentry defined, 121
Public relations:
    definition, 121
    description, 50-52
    occupation, 133-135
Publicity defined, 120
Publishing, 49-50

Radio, 84-85, 87-88
Radio stations, 52-54
Reddick, DeWitt C., 219
Reed, William A., Jr., 75, 83, 86-87
Religion Newswriters Association, 216
Religious Journalism: Whence and Whither? (Stoody), 126, 128
Religious journalist defined, 14-15
Religious News Service, 92, 97-100
Religious Public Relations Council, 217
Rex, Frederick, 152
Riley, Ruth E., 75
Robertson, Bruce L., quoted, 206, 213
Root, Robert W., 176-180, 220
Royer, Howard, 217
Ruff, G. Elson, 38, 94, 95
Runge, David A., 39

Sadler, Wesley, quoted, 152
Salaries, 223-224

Sayers, Dorothy L., quoted, 20
Schmitz, Charles, 39
Scholarships, 215-216
Schrock, Simon, 53
Secretarial work, 229-231
Semands, Ruth, 150
Settle, Paul G., quoted, 62, 206
Seventh-day Adventists, 125-126, 151
Shacklock, Floyd, 152
Shipler, Guy Emery, 95
Shoemaker, Dennis, 217
Shultz, Lee, quoted, 215
Skillen, Edward S., 94
Smith, Roy.L., quoted, 106-110
Soth, Connie, 177-179
Southern Baptist Press Association, 216
Spaid, Ora, 39, 75
Specializing, 190-192
Spence, Hartzell, 176
Spencer, M. Lyle, 141
Stauderman, Alfred P., 94
Stewart, Ford, 93
Stewart, Frank, 75
Stewart, John T., 75
Stoody, Ralph, 39, 126-129
Story papers, 57-58
Street, Harold B., 152
Stuber, Stanley I., 39, 132
Suderman, Dale, quoted, 210, 211
Supple, James, 39
Sweazy, George E., quoted, 125

Taft, Adon, 75
Tanner, William F., 219
Television, 52-54, 84-85, 87-88
Theology, 107
Thomas, Willa, 84
Thorkelson, Willmar L., 39, 75, 78
Thrapp, Dan L., 75
Tomkins, Leona, 84
Training, 48, 55-56, 204-207
Trexler, Edgar, 197-198
Tucker, Irwin St. John, 175

Index

Unions, 228-229
United Press International, 52

Van Horne, Marion, 152
Vance, Margaret A., 39, 75
Vocabulary, 103
Vocations in religion, 19-21
Volunteer service, 209-211

Wager, Richard, 75
Wall, James M., 94
Walker, Robert, 152
Walters, Samuel, 53
Ward, Hiley, 75
Waybill, Nelson, quoted, 205-206
West, Arthur, 39, 129-130
Whitaker, Robert, 75
White, Peter Gordon, quoted, 222

Widgeon, Pat, 84
Wiebe, Walter, quoted, 219
Williams, Michael, 94
Wilson, Dorothy Clarke, 184-185
Wilson, Kenneth, 39, 93
Workshops, 209-211
World Association for Christian Communication, 218
World Council of Churches, 51
World Over Press, 180
Woodward, Robert, 91
Wyn, John Charles, 220

Yates, Elizabeth, 185-186
Yost, F. Donald, 210

Zavistz, Lance, 75

Roland E. Wolseley is professor emeritus of journalism at the School of Public Communications, Syracuse University.

Educated in schools in New York, New Jersey, and Pennsylvania and at Northwestern University, from which he has two degrees in journalism, he worked on dailies in Pennsylvania and Illinois, did corporate public relations writing and editing, and publicity work for various church bodies.

He taught for eleven years at Northwestern before going to Syracuse University and has been on the faculty for shorter periods at Mundelein College, Nagpur University (India), and other institutions. He headed the Magazine Department at Syracuse for twenty-two years, the time during which its Religious Journalism Program was conducted under his direction. He also has been on the faculties of various religious and secular writer's conferences.

A free-lance writer since his early college days, he has published more than six hundred articles in about two hundred different publications, mostly magazines, in the United States, Canada, India, and the United Kingdom, including *Saturday Review, The Nation, Christian Century, Commonweal, Christian Science Monitor, Washington Post, The Churchman, The Lutheran*, and many periodicals for young people.

Professor Wolseley is author or coauthor of a score of books, including *Understanding Magazines, The Black Press, U.S.A., Writing for the Religious Market, Interpreting the Church Through Press and Radio, The Changing Magazine, Gandhi: Warrior of Non-Violence*, and *The Low Countries*.

A member of the United Methodist Church, he has led editorial workshops for that denomination as well as for the Southern Baptist Convention, the Lutheran Church in America, the General Conference Mennonite Church, the Associated Church Press, and the Evangelical Press Association.